# A Very Woman by Philip Massinger

## or, The Prince of Tarent

Philip Massinger was baptized at St. Thomas's in Salisbury on November 24th, 1583.

Massinger is described in his matriculation entry at St. Alban Hall, Oxford (1602), as the son of a gentleman. His father, who had also been educated there, was a member of parliament, and attached to the household of Henry Herbert, 2nd Earl of Pembroke. The Earl was later seen as a potential patron for Massinger.

He left Oxford in 1606 without a degree. His father had died in 1603, and accounts suggest that Massinger was left with no financial support this, together with rumours that he had converted to Catholicism, meant the next stage of his career needed to provide an income.

Massinger went to London to make his living as a dramatist, but he is only recorded as author some fifteen years later, when The Virgin Martyr (1621) is given as the work of Massinger and Thomas Dekker.

During those early years as a playwright he wrote for the Elizabethan stage entrepreneur, Philip Henslowe. It was a difficult existence. Poverty was always close and there was constant pleading for advance payments on forthcoming works merely to survive.

After Henslowe died in 1616 Massinger and John Fletcher began to write primarily for the King's Men and Massinger would write regularly for them until his death.

The tone of the dedications in later plays suggests evidence of his continued poverty. In the preface of The Maid of Honour (1632) he wrote, addressing Sir Francis Foljambe and Sir Thomas Bland: "I had not to this time subsisted, but that I was supported by your frequent courtesies and favours."

The prologue to The Guardian (1633) refers to two unsuccessful plays and two years of silence, when the author feared he had lost popular favour although, from the little evidence that survives, it also seems he had involved some of his plays with political characters which would have cast shadows upon England's alliances.

Philip Massinger died suddenly at his house near the Globe Theatre on March 17th, 1640. He was buried the next day in the churchyard of St. Saviour's, Southwark, on March 18th, 1640. In the entry in the parish register he is described as a "stranger," which, however, implies nothing more than that he belonged to another parish.

## Index of Contents

A VERY WOMAN or, THE PRINCE OF TARENT

DRAMATIS PERSONSAE
Viceroy of Sicily.
Don Pedro, his son.
Duke of Messina.
Don Martino Cardenes, his son.
Don John Antonio, Prince of Tarent.
Captain of the castle Palermo.
Paulo, a physician.
Cuculo, the Viceroy's Steward.
Two Surgeons.
Apothecary.
Citizens.
Slave-merchant.
Servant.
Page.
An English Slave.
Slaves.
Moors.

Pirates.
Sailors.
Almira, the Viceroy s daughter.
Leonora, duke of Messina's niece.
Borachia, wife to Cuculo, governess of Leonora and Almira.
Two Waiting Women.
A good and evil Genius, Servants, Guard, Attendants, & etc.


SCENE: Palermo


PROLOGUE

To such, and some there are, no question, here,
Who, happy in their memories do bear
This subject, long since acted, and can say,
Truly, -we have seen something like this play.
Our author, with becoming modesty,
(For in this kind he ne'er was bold,) by me,
In his defence thus answers, By command,
He undertook this task, nor could it stand
With his low fortune to refuse to do
What, by his patron, he was call'd unto:
For whose delight and yours, we hope, with care
He hath review d it; and with him we dare
Maintain to any man, that did allow
'Twos good before, it is much better' d now:
A r or is it, sure, against the proclamation
To raise new piles upon an old foundation.
So much to them deliver d; to the rest,
To whom each scene is fresh, he doth protest,
Should his Muse fail now a fair flight to make,
He cannot fancy what will please or take.


ACT I

SCENE I. A Room in the Viceroy's Palace

Enter **PEDRO** meeting **LEONORA**.

**PEDRO**
My worthiest mistress!
This day cannot end
But prosperous to Pedro, that begins
With this so wish'd encounter.

**LEONORA**
Only servant,
To give you thanks in your own courtly

[Enter **PEDRO** meeting **LEONORA**. language,

**PEDRO**
My worthiest mistress! this day
Would argue me more ceremonious cannot end
Than heartily affected; and you are
Too well assured, or I am miserable,
Our equal loves have kept one rank too long,
To stand at distance now.

**PEDRO**
You make me happy
In this so wise reproof, which I receive
As a chaste favour from you, and will ever
Hold such astrong command o'ermy desires,
That though my blood turn rebel to my reason,
I never shall presume to seek aught from you,
But what (your honour safe) you well may grant me,
And virtue sign the warrant.

**LEONORA**
Your love to me
So limited, will still preserve your mistress
Worthy her servant, and in your restraint
Of loose affections, bind me faster to you:
But there will be a time when we may welcome
Those wish'd for pleasures, as heaven's greatest blessings,
When that the viceroy, your most noble father,
And the duke my uncle, and to that, my riardian,
By their free consent confirm them lawful.

**PEDRO**
You ever shall direct, and I obey you:
Is my sister stirring yet?

**LEONORA**
Long since.

**PEDRO**
Some business
With her, join'd to my service to yourself,
Hath brought me hither; pray you vouchsafe the favour
To acquaint her with so much.

**LEONORA**
I am prevented.

[Enter **ALMIRA**, and **TWO WAITING-WOMEN** dressing her.

**ALMIRA**
Do the rest here, my cabinet is too hot;
This room is cooler. Brother!

**PEDRO**
Morrow, sister!
Do I not come unseasonably?

**ALMIRA**
Why, good brother?

**PEDRO**
Because you are not yet fully made up,
Nor fit for visitation. There are ladies,
And great ones, that will hardly grant access,
On any terms, to their own fathers, as
They are themselves, nor willingly be seen
Before they have ask'd counsel of their doctor
How the ceruse will appear, newly laid on,
When they ask blessing.

**ALMIRA**
Such, indeed, there are
That would be still young, in despite of time;
That in the wrinkled winter of their age
Would force a seeming April of fresh beauty,
As if it were within the power of art
To frame a second nature: but for me,
And for your mistress I dare say as much,
The faces, and the teeth you s'ee, we slept with.

**PEDRO**
Which is not frequent, sister, with some ladies.

**ALMIRA**
You spy no sign of any night-mask here,
(Tie on my carcanet,) nor does your nostril
Take in the scent of strong perfumes, to stifle
The sourness of our breaths as we are fasting:
You're in a lady's chamber, gentle brother,
And not in your apothecary's shop.
We use the women, you perceive, that serve us,
Like servants, not like such as do create us:

Faith, search our pockets, and, if you find there
Comfits of ambergris to help our kisses,
Conclude us faulty.

**PEDRO**
You are pleasant, sister,
And I am glad to find you so disposed;
You will the better hear me.

**ALMIRA**
What you please, sir.

**PEDRO**
I am entreated by the prince of
Tarent,
Don John Antonio

**ALMIRA**
Would you would choose
Some other subject.

**PEDRO**
Pray you, give me leave,
For his desires are fit for you to hear,
As for me to prefer. This prince of Tarent
(Let it not wrong him that I call him friend)
Finding your choice of don Cardenes liked of
By both your fathers, and his hopes cut off,
Resolves to leave Palermo.

**ALMIRA**
He does well;
That I hear gladly.

**PEDRO**
How this prince came hither,
How bravely furnish 'd, how attended on,
How he hath borne himself here, with what charge
He hath continued; his magnificence
In costly banquets, curious masques, rare presents,
And of all sorts, you cannot but remember.

**ALMIRA**
Give me my gloves.

**PEDRO**
Now, for reward of all
His cost, his travel, and his duteous service,

He does entreat that you will please he may
Take his leave of you, and receive the favour
Of kissing of your hands.

**ALMIRA**
You are his friend,
And shall dischaige the part of one to tell him
That he may spare the trouble; I desire not
To see or hear more of him.

**PEDRO**
Yet grant this,
Which a mere stranger, in the way of courtship,
Might challenge from you.

**ALMIRA**
And obtain it sooner.

**PEDRO**
One reason for this would do well.

**ALMIRA**
My will
Shall now stand for a thousand. Shall I lose
The privilege of my sex, which is my will,
To yield a reason like a man? or you,
Deny your sister that which all true women
Claim as their first prerogative, which nature
Gave to them for a law, and should I break it,
I were no more a woman?

**PEDRO**
Sure, a good one
You cannot be, if you put off that virtue
Which best adonis a good one, courtesy
And affable behaviour. Do not flatter'
Yourself with the opinion that your birth,
Your beauty, or whatever false 'ground else
You raise your pride upon, will stand against
The censure of just men.

**ALMIRA**
Why, let it fall then;
I still shall be unmoved.

**LEONORA**
And, pray you, be you so.
[Aside to **PEDRO**

**ALMIRA**
What jewel's that?

**LEONORA**
That which the prince of
Tarent

**ALMIRA**
Left here, and you received without my knowledge! '
I have use oft now. Does the page wait without,
My lord Cardenes sent to inquire my health?

**WAITING-WOMAN**
Yes, madam.

**ALMIRA**
Give it him, and, with it, pray him
To return my sendee to his lord, and mine.

**PEDRO**
Will you so undervalue one that has
So truly loved you, to bestow the pledge
Of his affection, being a prince, upon
The servant of his rival?

**LEONORA**
'Tis not well.
Faith, wear it, lady: send gold to the boy,
Twill please him better.

**ALMIRA**
Do as I command you.

[Exit **WAITING-WOMAN**.

I will keep nothing that may put me in mind
Don John Antonio ever loved, or was;
Being wholly now Cardenes.

**PEDRO**
In another
This were mere barbarism, sister; and in you,
For' I'll not sooth you,) at the best, 'tis rudeness.

**ALMIRA**
Rudeness!

**PEDRO**

Yes, rudeness; and, what's worse, the want
Of civil manners; nay, ingratitude
Unto the many and so fair deservings
Of don Antonio. Does this express
Your breeding in the court, or that you call
The viceroy father? a poor peasant's daughter,
That ne'er had conversation but with beasts,
Or men bred like them, would not so far shame
Her education.

**ALMIRA**

Pray you, leave my chamber;
I know you for a brother, not a tutor.
You are too violent, madam.

**ALMIRA**

Were my father
Here to command me, (as you take upon you
Almost to play his part,) I would refuse it.
Where I love, I profess it; where I hate,
In ever)' circumstance I dare proclaim it.
Of all that wear the shapes of men, I loath
That prince you plead for; no antipathy
Between things most averse in nature, holds
A stronger enmity than his with mine;
With which rest satisfied: If not, your anger
May wrong yourself, not me.

**LEONORA**

My lord Cardenes!

**PEDRO**

Go: in soft terms, if you persist thus, you
Will be one

[Enter **CARDENES**.

**ALMIRA**

What one? pray you, out with it.

**PEDRO**

Why, one that I shall wish a stranger to me,
That I might curse you; but—

**CARDENES**

Whence grows this heat?

**PEDRO**

Be yet advised, and entertain him fairly,
For I will send him to you; or no more
Know me a brother.

**ALMIRA**

As you please.

**PEDRO**

Good morrow.

[Exit.

**CARDENES**

Good morrow, and part thus! you seem moved too:
What desperate fool durst raise a tempest here,
To sink himself?

**ALMIRA**

Good sir, have patience;
The cause, though I confess I am not pleased,
No way deserves your anger.

**CARDENES**

Not mine, madam,
As if the least offence could point at you,
And I not feel it: as you have vouchsafed me
The promise of your heart, conceal it not,
Whomsoever it concerns.

**ALMIRA**

It is not worth
So serious an inquiry: my kind brother
Had a desire to learn me some new courtship,
Which I distasted; that was all.

**CARDENES**

Your brother!
In being yours, with more security
He might provoke you; yet, if he hath past
A brother's bounds

**LEONORA**

What then, my lord?

**CARDENES**

Believe it,
I'll call him to accompt for't.

**LEONORA**
Tell him so.

**ALMIRA**
No more.

**LEONORA**
Yes, thus much; though my modesty
Be call'd in question for it, in his absence
I will defend him: he hath said nor done,
But what don Pedro well might say or do;
Mark me, don Pedro! in which understand
As worthy, and as well as can be hoped for
Of those that love him best from don
Cardenes.

**CARDENES**
This to me, cousin!

**ALMIRA**
You forget 'yourself.

**LEONORA**
No, nor the cause in which you did so, lady,
'Which is so just that it needs no concealing
On Pedro's part.

**ALMIRA**
What mean you?

**LEONORA**
I dare speak it,
If you dare hear it, sir: he did persuade
Amira, your Almira, to vouchsafe
Some little conference with the prince of
Tarent,
Before he left the court; and, that the world
Might take some notice, though he prosper'd not
In his so loved design, he was not scorn'd,
He did desire the kissing of her hand,
And then to leave her: this was much!

**CARDENES**
'Twas more
Than should have been urged by him; well denied,
On your part, madam, and I thank you for't.
Antonio had his answer, I your grant;

And why your brother should prepare for him
An after-interview, or private favour,
I can find little reason.

**LEONORA**
None at all,
Why you should be displeased with't.

**CARDENES**
His respect
To me, as. things now are, should have weigh 'd down
His former friendship: 'twas done indiscreetly,
I would be loath to say, maliciously,
To build up the demolish 'd hopes of him
That was my rival. What had he to do,
If he view not my happiness in your favour
With wounded eyes, to take upon himself
An office so distasteful?

**LEONORA**
You may ask
As well, what any gentleman has to do
With civil courtesy.

**ALMIRA**
Or you, with that
Which at no part concerns you. Good my lord,
Rest satisfied, that I saw him not, nor will;
And that nor father, brother, nor the world,
Can work me unto anything but what
You give allowance to in which assurance,
With this, I leave you.

**LEONORA**
Nay, take me along;
You are not angry too?

**ALMIRA**
Presume on that.

[Exit, followed by **LEONORA**.

**CARDENES**
Am I assured of her, and shall again
Be tortured with suspicion to lose her,
Before I have enjoy' d her! the next sun
Shall see her mine; why should I doubt, then? yet,
To doubt is safer than to be secure.

But one short day! Great empires in less time
Have suffer'd change: she's constant but a woman;
And what a lover's vows, persuasions, tears,
May, in a minute, work upon such frailty,
There are too many and too sad examples.
The prince of Tarent gone, all were in safety;
Or not admitted to solicit her,
My fears would quit me: 'tis my fault, if I
Give way to that; and let him ne'er desire
To own what's hard to win, that dares not guard it.
Who waits there?

[Enter **SERVANTS** and **PAGE**.

**SERVANT**
Would your lordship aught?

**CARDENES**
'Tis well
You are so near.

[Enter **ANTONIO** and a **SERVANT**.

**ANTONIO**
Take care all things be ready
For my remove.

**SERVANT**
They are.

[Exit.

**CARDENES**
We meet like friends,
No more like rivals now: my emulation
Puts on the shape of love and service to you.

**ANTONIO**
It is return'd.

**CARDENES**
'Twas rumoured in the court
You were to leave the city, and that won me
To find you out. Your excellence may wonder
That I, that never saw you, till this hour,
But that I wish'd you dead, so willingly
Should come to wait upon you to the ports;
And there, with hope you never will look back,

Take my last farewell of you.

**ANTONIO**
'Never look back'!

**CARDENES**
I said so; neither is it fit you should;
And may I prevail with you as a friend,
You never shall; nor, while you live, hereafter
Think of the viceroy's court, or of Palermo,
But as a grave, in which the prince of Tarent
Buried his honour.

**ANTONIO**
You speak in a language
I do not understand.

**CARDENES**
No! I'll be plainer.
What madman, that came hither with that pomp
Don John Antonio did, that exact courtier
Don John Antonio, with whose brave fame only
Great princesses have fall'n in love, and died;
That came with such assurance, as young Paris
Did to fetch Helen, being sent back, contemn'd,
Disgraced, and scora'd, his large expense laugh 'd at,
His braver.' scoff d, the lady that he courted
Left quietly in possession of another,
(Not to be named that day a courtier
Where he was mention'd,) the scarce-known
Cardenes,
And he to bear her from him! that would ever
Be seen again (having got fairly off)
By such as will live ready witnesses
Of his repulse and scandal?

**ANTONIO**
The grief of it,
Believe me, will not kill me: all man's honour
Depends not on the most uncertain favour
Of a fair mistress.

**CARDENES**
Troth, you bear it well.
You should have seen some that were sensible
Of a disgrace, that would have raged, and sought
To cure their honour with some strange revenge:
But you are better temper'd; and they wrong

The Neapolitans in their report,
That say they are fiery spirits, uncapable
Of the least injury, dangerous to be talk'd with
After a loss; where nothing can move you,
But, like a stoic, with a constancy
Words nor affronts can shake, you still go on,
And smile when men abuse you.

**ANTONIO**
If they wrong
Themselves,
I would have yon know,
I dare be angry.

**CARDENES**
Tis not possible.
A taste oft would do well; and I'd make trial
What may be done.
Come hither, boy. You have seen
This jewel, as I take it?

**ANTONIO**
Yes; 'tis that
I gave Almira.

**CARDENES**
And in what esteem
She held it, coming from your worthy self,
You may perceive, that freely hath bestow'd it
Upon my page.

**ANTONIO**
When I presented it,
I did not indent with her, to what use
She should employ it.

**CARDENES**
See the kindness of
A loving soul! who, after this neglect,
Nay, gross contempt, will look again upon her,
And not be frighted from it.

**ANTONIO**
No, indeed, sir;
Nor give way longer give way, do you mark,
To your loose wit, to run the wild-goose chase,
Six syllables further. I will see the lady,
That lady that dotes on you, from whose hate

My love increases, though you stand elected
Her porter, to deny me.

**CARDENES**
Sure you will not.

**ANTONIO**
Yes, instantly: your prosperous success
Hath made you insolent; and for her sake
I have thus long forborne you, and can yet
Forget it and forgive it, ever provided,
That you end here; and, for what's past recalling,
That she make intercession for your pardon,
Which, at her suit, I'll grant.

**CARDENES**
I am much unwilling
To move her for a trifle bear that too,

[Strikes him.

And then she shall speak to you.

**ANTONIO**
Men and angels,
Take witness for me, that I have endured
More than a man!

[They fight; **CARDENES** falls.

O do not fall so soon,
Stand up take my hand so! when I have printed,
For every contumelious word, a wound here,
Then sink for ever.

**CARDENES**
Oh, I suffer justly!

**1ST SERVANT**
Murder! murder! murder!

[Exit.

**2ND SERVANT**
Apprehend him.

**3RD SERVANT**
We'll all join with you.

**ANTONIO**
I do wish you more;
My fury will be lost else, if it meet not
Matter to work on: one life is too little
For so much injury.

[Re-enter **ALMIRA**, **LEONORA**, and **SERVANT**.

**ALMIRA**
O my Cardenes!
Though dead, still my Cardenes! Villains, cowards,
What do ye check at? can one arm, and that
A murderer's, so long guard the curs'd master,
Against so many swords made sharp with justice?

**1ST SERVANT**
Sure he will kill us all; he is a devil.

**2ND SERVANT**
He is invulnerable.

**ALMIRA**
Your base fears
Beget such fancies in you. Give me a sword,

[Snatches a sword from the **SERVANT**.

This my weak arm, made strong in my revenge,
Shall force a way to't.

[Wounds **ANTONIO**.

**ANTONIO**
Would it were deeper, madam!
The thrust, which I would not put by, being yours,
Of greater force, to have pierced through that heart
Which still retains your figure! weep still, lady;
For every tear that flows from those grieved eyes,
Some part of that which maintains life, goes from me;
And so to die were in a gentle slumber
To pass to paradise: but you envy me
So quiet a departure from my world,
My world of miseries; therefore, take my sword,
And, having kill'd me with it, cure the wounds
It gave Cardenes.

[Gives **ALMIRA** his sword.

[Re-enter **PEDRO**.

**PEDRO**
'Tis too true was ever
Valour so ill employed!

**ANTONIO**
Why stay you, lady?
Let not soft pity work on your hard nature;
You cannot do a better office to
The dead Cardenes, and I willingly
Shall fall a ready sacrifice to appease him,
Your fair hand offering it.

**ALMIRA**
Thou couldst ask nothing
But this, which I would grant.

[Attempts to wound him.

**LEONORA**
Flint-hearted lady!

**PEDRO**
Are you a woman, sister!

[Takes the sword from her.

**ALMIRA**
Thou art not
A brother, I renounce that title to thee;
Thy hand is in this bloody act; 'twas this,
For which that savage homicide was sent hither.
Thou equal Judge of all things! if that blood,
And innocent blood

**PEDRO**
Best sister.

**ALMIRA**
Oh, Cardenes!
How is my soul rent between rage and sorrow,
That it can be that such an upright cedar
Should violently be torn up by the roots,
Without an earthquake in that very moment
To swallow them that did it!

**ANTONIO**
The hurt's nothing;
But the deep wound is in my conscience, friend,
Which sorrow in death only can recover.

**PEDRO**
Have better hopes.

[Enter **VICEROY**, **DUKE of MESSINA**, **CAPTAIN**, **GUARD**, and **SERVANTS**.

**DUKE of MESSINA**
My son, is this the marriage
I came to celebrate? false hopes of man!
I come to find a grave here.

**ALMIRA**
I have wasted
My stock of tears, and now just anger help me
To pay, in my revenge, the other part
Of duty, which I owe thee. O, great sir,
Not as a daughter now, but a poor widow,
Made so before she was a bride, I fly
To your impartial justice: the offence
Is death, and death in his most horrid form;
Let not, then, title, or a prince's name,
(Since a great crime is, in a great man, greater,)
Secure the offender.

**DUKE of MESSINA**
Give me life for life,
As thou wilt answer it to the great king,
Whose deputy thou art here.

**ALMIRA**
And speedy justice.

**DUKE of MESSINA**
Put the damn'd wretch to torture.

**ALMIRA**
Force him to
Reveal his curs'd confederates, which spare not,
Although you find a son among them.

**VICEROY**
How!

**DUKE of MESSINA**

Why bring you not the rack forth?

**ALMIRA**
Wherefore stands
The murderer unbound?

**VICEROY**
Shall I have hearing?

**DUKE of MESSINA**
Excellent lady, in this you express
Your true love to the dead.

**ALMIRA**
All love to mankind
From me, ends with him.

**VICEROY**
Will you hear me yet?
And first to you; you do confess the fact
With which you stand charged?

**ANTONIO**
I will not make worse
What is already ill, with vain denial.

**VICEROY**
Then understand, though you are prince of Tarent,
Yet, being a subject to the king of Spain,
No privilege of Sicily can free you
(Being convict by a just form of law)
From the municipal statutes oi that kingdom,
But as a common man, being found guilty,
Must suffer for it.

**ANTONIO**
I prize not my life
So much, as to appeal from anything
You shall determine of me.

**VICEROY**
Yet despair not
To have an equal hearing; the exclaims
Of this grieved father, nor my daughter's tears,
Shall sway me from myself; and, where they urge
To have you tortured, or led bound to prison,
I must not grant it.

**DUKE of MESSINA**
No!

**VICEROY**
I cannot, sir;
For men of his rank are to be distinguish 'd
From other men, before they are condemn'd,
From which (his cause not heard) he yet stands free:
So take him to your charge, and, as your life,
See he be safe.

**CAPTAIN**
Let me die for him else.

[Exeunt **PEDRO**, and **CAPTAIN** and **GUARD** with **ANTONIO**.

**DUKE of MESSINA**
The guard of him should have been given to me.

**ALMIRA**
Or unto me.

**DUKE of MESSINA**
Bribes may corrupt the captain.

**ALMIRA**
And our just wreak, by force, or cunning practice,
With scorn prevented.

**CARDENES**
Oh!

**ALMIRA**
What groan is that?

**VICEROY**
There are apparent signs of life yet in him.

**ALMIRA**
Oh that there were! that I could pour my blood
Into his veins!

**CARDENES**
Oh, oh!

**VICEROY**
Take him up gently.

**DUKE of MESSINA**
Run for physicians.

**ALMIRA**
Surgeons.

**DUKE of MESSINA**
All helps else.

**VICEROY**
This care of his recovery, timely practised,
Would have express'd more of a father in you,
Than your impetuous clamours for revenge.
But I shall find fit time to urge that further,
Hereafter, to you; 'tis not fit for me
To add weight to oppress 'd calamity.

[Exeunt.


ACT II

SCENE I. A Room in the Castle

Enter **PEDRO, ANTONIO,** and **CAPTAIN**.

**ANTONIO**
Why should) our love to me, having already
So oft endured the test, be put unto
A needless trial? have you not, long since,
In every circumstance and rite of friendship,
Out gone all precedents the ancients boast of.
And will you yet move further?

**PEDRO**
Hitherto
I have done nothing (howsoe'er you value
My weak endeavours) that may justly claim
A title to your friendship, and much less
Laid down the debt, which, as a tribute due
To your deservings not I, but mankind
Stands bound to tender.

**ANTONIO**
Do not make an idol
Of him that should, and without superstition,
To you build up an altar. O my Pedro!

When I am to expire, to call you mine,
Assures a future happiness: give me leave
To argue with you, and, the fondness of
Affection struck blind, with justice hear me:
Why should you, being innocent, fling your life
Into the furnace of your father's anger,
For my offence? or, take it granted (yet
Tis more than supposition) you prefer
My safety 'fore your own, so prodigally
You waste your favours, wherefore should this captain,
His blood and sweat rewarded in the favour
Of his great master, falsify the trust
Which, from true judgment, he reposes in him,
For me a stranger?

**PEDRO**
Let him answer that,
He needs no prompter: speak your thoughts, and freely.

**CAPTAIN**
I ever loved to do so, and it shames not
The bluntness of my breeding: from my youth
I was train'd up a soldier, one of those
That in their natures love the dangers more,
Than the rewards of danger. I could add,
My life, when forfeited, the viceroy pardon'd
But by his intercession; and therefore,
It being lent by him, I were ungrateful,
Which I will never be, if I refused
To pay that debt at any time demanded.

**PEDRO**
I hope, friend, this will satisfy you.

**ANTONIO**
No, it raises
More doubts within me. Shall I, from the School
Of gratitude, in which this captain reads
The text so plainly, learn to be unthankful?
Or, viewing in your actions the idea
Of perfect friendship, when it does point to me
How brave a thing it is to be a friend,
Turn from the object? Had I never loved
The fair Almira for her outward features,
Nay, were the beauties of her mind suspected,
And her contempt and scorn painted before me,
The being your sister would anew inflame me,
With much more impotence to dote upon her:

No, dear friend, let me in my death confirm,
(Though you in all things else have the precedence,)
I'll die ten times, ere one of Pedro's hairs
Shall suffer in my cause.

**PEDRO**
If you so love me,
In love to that part of my soul dwells in you,
(For though two bodies, friends have but one soul,)
Lose not both life and me.

[Enter a **SERVANT**.

**SERVANT**
The prince is dead,

[Exit.

**ANTONIO**
If so, shall I leave Pedro here to answer
For my escape? as thus I clasp thee, let
The viceroy's sentence find me.

**PEDRO**
Fly, for heaven's sake!
Consider the necessity; though now
We part, Antonio, we may meet again,
But death's division is for ever, friend.

[Enter another **SERVANT**.

**SERVANT**
The rumour spread, sir, of Martino's death,
Is check'd j there's hope of his recovery.

[Exit.

**ANTONIO**
Why should I fly, then, when I may enjoy,
With mine own life, my friend?

**PEDRO**
That's still uncertain,
He may have a relapse; for once be ruled, friend:
He's a good debtor that pays when 'tis due;
A prodigal, that, before it is required,
Makes tender of it.

[Enter **SAILORS**.

**1ST SAILOR**
The bark, sir, is ready.

**2ND SAILOR**
The wind sits fair.

**3RD SAILOR**
Heaven favours your escape.

[Whistles within.

**CAPTAIN**
Hark, how the boatswain whistles you aboard!
Will nothing move you?

**ANTONIO**
Can I leave my friend?

**PEDRO**
I must delay no longer; force him hence.

**CAPTAIN**
I'll run the hazard of my fortunes with you.

**ANTONIO**
What violence is this? hear but my reasons.

**PEDRO**
Poor friendship that is cool'd with arguments!
Away, away!

**CAPTAIN**
For Malta.

**PEDRO**
You shall hear
All our events.

**ANTONIO**
I may sail round the world,
But never meet thy like. Pedro!

**PEDRO**
Antonio!

**ANTONIO**

I breathe my soul back to thee.

**PEDRO**
In exchange,
Bear mine along with thee.

**CAPTAIN**
Cheerly, my hearts!

[Exeunt **CAPTAIN** and **SAILORS** with **ANTONIO**.

**PEDRO**
He's gone: may pitying heaven his pilot be,
And then I weigh not what becomes of me.

[Exit.


SCENE II. A Room in the Viceroy's Palace

Enter **VICEROY**, **DUKE of MESSINA**, and **ATTENDANTS**.

**VICEROY**
I tell you right, sir.

**DUKE of MESSINA**
Yes, like a rough surgeon,
Without a feeling in yourself you search
My wounds unto the quick, then pre-declare,
The tediousness and danger of the cure,
Never remembering what the patient suffers
But you preach this philosophy to a man
That does partake of passion, and not
To a dull stoic.

**VICEROY**
I confess you have
Just cause to mourn your son; and yet, if reason
Cannot yield comfort, let example cure.
I am a father too, my only daughter
As dear in my esteem, perhaps as worthy,
As your Martino, in her love to him
As desperately ill, cither's loss equal;
And yet I bear it with a better temper:

[Enter **PEDRO**

Which, if you please to imitate, 'twill not wrong
Your piety, nor your judgment.

**DUKE of MESSINA**
We were fashion'd
In different moulds. I weep with mine own eyes, sir,
Pursue my ends too; pity to you's a cordial,
Revenge to me; and that I must and will have,
If my Martino die.

**PEDRO**
Your must and it'ill,
Shall in your full-sailed confidence deceive you. [Aside.
Here's doctor Paulo, sir.

[Enter **PAULO** and **TWO SURGEONS**.

**DUKE of MESSINA**
My hand! you rather
Deserve my knee, and it shall bend as to
A second father, if your saving aids
Restore my son.

**VICEROY**
Rise, thou bright star of knowledge,
Thou honour of thy art, thou help of nature,
Thou glory of our academies!

**PAULO**
If I blush, sir,
To hear these attributes ill-placed on me,
It is excusable. I am no god, sir,
Nor holy saint that can do miracles,
But a weak, sinful man: yet, that I may,
In some proportion, deserve these favours
Your excellencies please to grace me with,
I promise all the skill I have acquired
In simples, or the careful observation
Of the superior bodies, with my judgment
Derived from long experience, stand ready
To do you service.

**DUKE of MESSINA**
Modestly replied.

**VICEROY**
How is it with your princely patient?

**DUKE of MESSINA**
Speak,
But speak some comfort, sir.

**PAULO**
I must speak truth:
His wounds though many, heaven so guided yet
Antonio's sword, it pierced no part was mortal.
These gentlemen, who worthily deserve
The names of surgeons, have done their duties:
The means they practised, not ridiculous charms
To stop the blood; no oils, nor balsams bought
Of cheating quack-salvers, or mountebanks,
By them applied: the rules by Chiron taught,
And Æsculapius, which drew upon him
The Thunderer's envy, they with care pursued,
Heaven prospering their endeavours.

**DUKE of MESSINA**
There is hope, then,
Of his recovery?

**PAULO**
But no assurance;
I must not flatter you. That little air
Of comfort that breathes towards us (for I dare not
Rob these t 'enrich myself) you owe their care;
For, yet, I have done nothing.

**DUKE of MESSINA**
Still more modest;
I will begin with them: to either give
Three thousand crowns.

**VICEROY**
I'll double your reward:
See them paid presently.

**1ST SURGEON**
This magnificence
With equity cannot be conferr'd on us;
'Tis due unto the doctor.

**2ND SURGEON**
True; we were
But his subordinate ministers, and did only
Follow his grave directions.

**PAULO**
'Tis your own:
I challenge no part in it.

**VICEROY**
Brave on both sides!

**PAULO**
Deserve this, with the honour that will follow,
In your attendance.

**2ND SURGEON**
If both sleep at once,
'Tis justice both should die.

[Exeunt **SURGEONS**.

**DUKE of MESSINA**
For you, grave doctor,
We will not in such petty sums consider
Your high deserts; our treasury lies open,
Command it as your own.

**VICEROY**
Choose any castle,
Nav, citv, in our government, and be lord oft.

**PAULO**
Of neither, sir; I am not so ambitious:
Nor would I have your highnesses secure.
We have but faintly yet begun our journey;
A thousand difficulties and dangers must be
Encounter'd, ere we end it: though his hurts,
I mean his outward ones, do promise fair,
There is a deeper one, and in his mind,
Must be with care provided for; melancholy,
And at the height, too, near akin to madness,
Possesses him; his senses are distracted,
Not one, but all; and, if I can collect them,
With all the various ways invention
Or industry e'er practised, I shall write it
My masterpiece.

**DUKE of MESSINA**
You more and more engage me.

**VICEROY**
May we not visit him?

**PAULO**
By no means, sir;
As he is now, such courtesies come untimely:
I'll yield you reason fort. Should he look on you,
It will renew the memory of that
Which I would have forgotten; your good prayers
And those I do presume shall not be wanting
To my endeavours, are the utmost aids
I yet desire your excellencies should grant me.
So, with my humblest service

**DUKE of MESSINA**
Go, and prosper.

[Exit **PAULO**.

**VICEROY**
Observe his piety; I have heard, how true
I know not, most physicians, as they grow
Greater in skill, grow less in their religion;
Attributing so much to natural causes,
That they have little faith in that they cannot
Deliver reason for: this doctor steers
Another course but let this pass. If you please,
Your company to my daughter.

**DUKE of MESSINA**
I wait on you.

[Exeunt.


SCENE III. Another Room in the Same

Enter **LEONORA** and **WAITING-WOMEN**.

**LEONORA**
Took she no rest to-night?

**1ST WAITING-WOMAN**
Not any, madam;
I am sure she slept not. If she slumber'd, straight,
As if some dreadful vision had appear'd,
She started up, her hair unbound, and with
Distracted looks staring about the chamber,
She asks aloud, Where is Martina? where

Have you conceal' d him f sometimes names
Antonio,
Trembling in every joint, her brows contracted,
Her fair face as 'twere changed into a curse,
Her hands held up thus; and, as if her words
Were too big to find passage through her mouth,
She groans, then throws herself upon her bed,
Beating her breast.

**LEONORA**
'Tis wonderous strange.

**2ND WAITING-WOMAN**
Nay, more;
She that of late vouchsafed not to be seen,
But so adorn'd as if she were to rival
Nero's Poppaea, or the Egyptian queen,
Now, careless of her beauties, when we offer
Our service, she contemns it.

**LEONORA**
Does she not
Sometimes forsake her chamber?

**2ND WAITING-WOMAN**
Much about
This hour; then, with a strange unsettled gait,
She measures twice or thrice the gallery,
Silent, and frowning, (we dare not speak to her,)
And then returns. She's come, pray you, now observe her.

[Enter **ALMIRA** in black, carelessly habited.

**ALMIRA**
Why are my eyes fix'd on the ground, and not
Bent upwards? ha! that which was mortal of
My dear Martino, as a debt to nature,
I know this mother earth hath sepulchred;
But his diviner part, his soul, o'er which
The tyrant Death, nor yet the fatal sword
Of curs'd Antonio, his instrument,
Had the least power, borne upon angels' wings
Appointed to that office, mounted far
Above the firmament.

**LEONORA**
Strange imagination!
Dear cousin, your Martino lives.

**ALMIRA**
I know you,
And that in this you flatter me; he's dead,
As much as could die of him: but look yonder!
Amongst a million of glorious lights
That deck the heavenly canopy, I have
Discern 'd his soul, transform'd into a star.
Do you not see it?

**LEONORA**
Lady!

**ALMIRA**
Look with my eyes.
What splendour circles it! the heavenly archer,
Not far off distant, appears dim with envy,
Viewing himself outshined. Bright constellation!
Dart down thy beams of pity on Almira,
And, since thou find'st such grace where now thou art,
As I did truly love thee on the earth,
Like a kind harbinger, prepare my lodging,
And place me near thee!

**LEONORA**
I much more than fear
She'll grow into a frenzy.

**ALMIRA**
How? what's this!
A dismal sound! come nearer, cousin;
Your ear close to the ground, closer, you.
Do you howl? are you there, Antonio?

**LEONORA**
Where, sweet lady?

**ALMIRA**
In the vault, in hell, on the infernal rack,
Where murderers are tormented: yerk him soundly,
Twas Rhadamanth's sentence; do your office, Furies.
How he roars! What! plead to me to mediate for you!
I'm deaf, I cannot hear you.

**LEONORA**
'Tis but fancy,
Collect yourself.

**ALMIRA**
Leave babbling; 'tis rare music!
Rhamnusia plays on a pair of tongs
Red hot, and Proserpine dances to the consort;
Pluto sits laughing by too. So! enough:
I do begin to pity him.

**LEONORA**
I wish, madam,
You would shew it to yourself.

**2ND WAITING-WOMAN**
Her fit begins
To leave her.

**ALMIRA**
Oh my brains! are you there, cousin?

**LEONORA**
Now she speaks temperately. I am ever ready
To do you service': how do you?

**ALMIRA**
Very much troubled.
I have had the strangest waking dream of hell
And heaven I know not what.

**LEONORA**
My lord your father
Is come to visit you; as you would not grieve him
That is so tender of you, entertain him
With a becoming duty.

[Enter **VICEROY**, **DUKE of MESSINA**, **PEDRO**, and **ATTENDANTS**.

**VICEROY**
Still forlorn!
No comfort, my Almira?

**DUKE of MESSINA**
In your sorrow,
For my Martino, madam, you have express'd
All possible love and tenderness; too much of it
Will wrong yourself, and him. He may live, lady,
(For we are not past hope,) with his future service,
In some part to deserve it.

**ALMIRA**

If heaven please
To be so gracious to me, I will serve him
With such obedience, love, and humbleness,
That I will rise up an example for
Good wives to follow: but until I have
Assurance what fate will determine of me,
Thus, like a desolate widow, give me leave
To weep for him; for, should he die, I have vow'd
Not to outlive him; and my humble suit is,
One monument may cover us, and Antonio
(In justice you must grant me that) be offer'd
A sacrifice to our ashes.

**VICEROY**
Prithee put off
These sad thoughts; both shall live, I doubt it not,
A happy pair.

[Enter **CUCULO**, and **BORACHIA**.

**CUCULO**
O sir, the foulest treason
That ever was discover'd!

**VICEROY**
Speak it, that
We may prevent it.

**CUCULO**
Nay, 'tis past prevention:
Though you allow me wise, (in modesty,
I will not say oraculous,) I cannot help it.
I am a statesman, and some say a wise one;
But I could never conjure, nor divine
Of things to come.

**VICEROY**
Leave fooling: to the point;
What treason?

**CUCULO**
The false prince, don John Antonio,
Is fled.

**VICEROY**
It is not possible.

**PEDRO**

Peace, screech-owl.

**CUCULO**
I must speak, and it shall out, sir; the captain
You trusted with the fort is run away too.

**ALMIRA**
O miserable woman! I defy
All comfort: cheated too of my revenge!
As you are my father, sir, and you my brother,
I will not curse you; but I dare, and will say,
You are unjust and treacherous. If there be
A way to death, I'll find it.

[Exit.

**VICEROY**
Follow her,
She'll do some violent act upon herself;
Till she be better temper 'd, bind her hands.
And fetch the doctor to her.

[Exeunt **LEONORA**, and **WAITING-WOMEN**.

Had not you
A hand in this?

**PEDRO**
I, sir! I never knew
Such disobedience.

**VICEROY**
My honour's touch'd in't:
Let gallies be mann'd forth in his pursuit,
Search even' port and harbour; if I live,
He shall not 'scape thus.

**DUKE of MESSINA**
Fine hypocrisy!
Away, dissemblers! 'tis confederacy
Betwixt thy son, and self, and the false captain,
He could not thus have vanish'd else. You have murder'd
My son amongst you, and now murder justice:
You know it most impossible he should live,
Howe'er the doctor, for your ends, dissembled,
And you have shifted hence Antonio.

**VICEROY**

Messina, thou'rt a crazed and grieved old man,
And being in my court, protected by
The law of hospitality, or I should
Give you a sharper answer: may I perish,
If I knew of his flight!

**DUKE of MESSINA**
Fire, then, the castle.
Hang up the captain's wife and children.

**VICEROY**
Fie, sir!

**PEDRO**
My lord, you are uncharitable; capital treasons
Exact not so much.

**DUKE of MESSINA**
Thanks, most noble signior!
We ever had your good word and your love.

**CUCULO**
Sir, I dare pass my word, my lords are clear
Of any imputation in this case
You seem to load them with.

**DUKE of MESSINA**
Impertinent fool!
No, no; the loving faces you put on,
Have been but grinning visors: you have juggled me
Out of my son, and out of justice too;
But Spain shall do me right, believe me, Viceroy:
There I will force it from thee by the king.
He shall not eat nor sleep in peace for me,
Till I am righted for this treachery.

**VICEROY**
Thy worst, Messina! since no reason can
Qualify thy intemperance; the corruption
Of my subordinate ministers cannot wrong
My true integrity. Let privy searchers
Examine all the land.

**PEDRO**
Fair fall Antonio! [Aside.

[Exeunt **VICEROY**, **PEDRO**, and **ATTENDANTS**.

**CUCULO**
This is my wife, my lord; troth speak your conscience,
Is't not a goodly dame?

**DUKE of MESSINA**
She is no less, sir;
I will make use of these: may I entreat you
To call my niece.

**BORACHIA**
With speed, sir.

[Exit **BORACHIA**.

**CUCULO**
You may, my lord, suspect me
As an agent in these state-conveyances:
Let signior Cuculo, then, be never more,
For all his place, wit, and authority,
Held a most worthy, honest gentleman.

[Re-enter **BORACHIA** with **LEONORA**.

**DUKE of MESSINA**
I do acquit you, signior. Niece, you see
To what extremes I am driven; the cunning viceroy,
And his son Pedro, having express'd too plainly
Their cold affections to my son Martino:
And therefore I conjure thee, Leonora,
By all thy hopes from me, which is my dukedom
If my son fail, however, all thy fortunes;
Though heretofore some love hath past betwixt
Don Pedro, and thyself, abjure him now:
And as thou keep'st Almira company,
In this her desolation, so in hate
To this young Pedro, for thy cousin's love,
Be her associate; or assure thyself,
I cast thee like a stranger from my blood.
If I do ever hear thou see'st, or send'st
Token, or receiv'st message by yon heaven,
I never more will own thee!

**LEONORA**
O, dear uncle!
You have put a tyrannous yoke upon my heart,
And it will break it.

[Exit.

**DUKE of MESSINA**
Gravest lady, you
May be a great assister in my ends.
I buy your diligence thus: divide this couple,
Hinder their interviews; feign 'tis her will
To give him no admittance, if he crave it;
And thy rewards shall be thine own desires:
Whereto, good sir, but add your friendly aids,
And use me to my uttermost.

**CUCULO**
My lord,

If my wife please, I dare not contradict.
Borachia, what do you say?

**BORACHIA**
I say, my lord,
I know my place; and be assured, I will
Keep fire and tow asunder.

**DUKE of MESSINA**
You in this
Shall much deserve me.

[Exit.

**CUCULO**
We have ta'en upon us
A heavy charge: I hope you'll now forbear
The excess of wine.

**BORACHIA**
I will do what I please.
This day the market's kept for slaves; go you,
And buy me a fine-timber'd one to assist me;
I must be better waited on.

**CUCULO**
Anything,
So you'll leave wine.

**BORACHIA**
Still prating!

**CUCULO**
I am gone, duck.

[Exit.

**BORACHIA**
Pedro! so hot upon the scent! I'll fit him.

[Re-enter **PEDRO**.

**PEDRO**
Donna Borachia, you most happily
Are met to pleasure me.

**BORACHIA**
It may be so;
I use to pleasure many. Here lies my way,
I do beseech you, sir, keep on your voyage.

**PEDRO**
Be not so short, sweet lady, I must with you.

**BORACHIA**
With me, sir! I beseech you, sir why, what, sir,
See you in me?

**PEDRO**
Do not mistake me, lady;
Nothing but honesty.

**BORACHIA**
Hang honesty!
Trump me not up with honesty: do you mark, sir,
I have a charge, sir, and a special charge, sir,
And 'tis not honesty can win on me, sir.

**PEDRO**
Prithee conceive me rightly.

**BORACHIA**
I conceive you!

**PEDRO**
But understand.

**BORACHIA**
I will not understand, sir,
I cannot, nor I do not understand, sir.

**PEDRO**

Prithee, Borachia, let me see my mistress,
But look upon her; stand you by.

**BORACHIA**
How's this!
Shall I stand by? what do you think of me?
Now, by the virtue of the place I hold,
You are a paltry lord to tempt my trust thus:
I am no Helen, nor no Hecuba,
To be deflower'd of my loyalty
With your fair language.

**PEDRO**
Thou mistak'st me still.

**BORACHIA**
It may be so, my place will bear me out in't,
And will mistake you still, make you your best on't.

**PEDRO**
A pox upon thee! let me but behold her.

**BORACHIA**
A plague upon you! you shall never see her.

**PEDRO**
This is a crone in grain! thou art so testy
Prithee, take breath, and know thy friends.

**BORACHIA**
I will not,
I have no friends, nor I will have none this way:
And, now I think on't better, why will you see her?

**PEDRO**
Because she loves me dearly, I her equally.

**BORACHIA**
She hates you damnably, most wickedly,
Build that upon my word, most wickedly;
And swears her eyes are sick when they behold you.
How fearfully have I heard her rail upon you,
And cast and rail again; and cast again;
Call for hot waters, and then rail again!

**PEDRO**
How! 'tis not possible.

**BORACHIA**
I have heard her swear
(How justly, you best know, and where the cause lies)
That you are I shame to tell it but it must out
Fie, fie! why, how have you deserv'd it?

**PEDRO**
I am what?

**BORACHIA**
The beastliest man why, what a grief must this be?
(Sir-reverence of the company) a rank whoremaster:
Ten livery whores, she assured me on her credit,
With weeping eyes she spake it, and seven citizens,
Besides all voluntaries that serve under you,
And of all countries.

**PEDRO**
This must needs be a lie.

**BORACHIA**
Besides, you are so careless of your body,
Which is a foul fault in you.

**PEDRO**
Leave your fooling,
For this shall be a fable: happily,
My sister's anger may grow strong against me,
Which thou mistak'st.

**BORACHIA**
She hates you very well too,
But your mistress hates you heartily: look upon you!
Upon my conscience, she should see the devil first,
With eyes as big as saucers; when I but named you,
She has leap'd back thirty feet: if once she smell you,
For certainly you are rank, she says, extreme rank,
And the wind stand with you too, she's gone for ever!

**PEDRO**
For all this, I would see her.

**BORACHIA**
That's all one.
Have you new eyes when those are scratch'd out, or a nose
To clap on warm? have you proof against a piss-pot,
Which, if they bid me, I must fling upon you?

**PEDRO**
I shall not see her, then, you say?

**BORACHIA**
It seems so.

**PEDRO**
Prithee, be thus far friend then, good Borachia,
To give her but this letter, and this ring,
And leave thy pleasant lying, which I pardon:
But leave it in her pocket; there's no harm in't.
I'll take thee up a petticoat, will that please thee?

**BORACHIA**
Take up my petticoat! I scorn the motion,
I scorn it with my heels; take up my petticoat!

**PEDRO**
And why thus hot?

**BORACHIA**
Sir, you shall find me hotter,
If you take up my petticoat.

**PEDRO**
I'll give thee a new petticoat.

**BORACHIA**
I scorn the gift take up my petticoat!
Alas! my lord, you are too young, my lord,
Too young, my lord, to circumcise me that way.
Take up my petticoat! I am a woman,
A woman of another way, my lord,
A gentlewoman: he that takes up my petticoat,
Shall have enough to do, I warrant him,
I would fain see the proudest of you all so lusty.

**PEDRO**
Thou art disposed still to mistake me.

**BORACHIA**
Petticoat!
You shew now what you are; but do your worst, sir.

**PEDRO**
A wild-fire take thee!

**BORACHIA**

I ask no favour of you,
And so I leave you; and withal, I charge you
In my own name, for, sir, I'd have you know it,
Tn this place I present your father's person,
Upon your life, not dare to follow me,
For if you do

[Exit.

**PEDRO**
Go! and the pox go with thee,
If thou hast so much moisture to receive them!
For thou wilt have them, though a horse bestow them.
I must devise a way for I must see her,
And very suddenly; and, madam petticoat,
If all the wit I have, and this can do,
I'll make you break your charge, and your hope too.

[Exit.


ACT III

SCENE I. The Slave Market

Enter **SLAVE-MERCHANT** and **SERVANT**, with **ANTONIO** and **CAPTAIN** disguised, and dressed as Slaves, **ENGLISH SLAVE**, and **DIVERS**, other **SLAVES**.

**SLAVE-MERCHANT**
Come, rank yourselves, and stand out handsomely.
Now ring the bell, that they may know my market.
Stand you two here; [To **ANTONIO** and the **CAPTAIN**] you are personable men,
And apt to yield good sums, if women cheapen.
Put me that pig-complexion'd fellow behind,
He will spoil my sale else; the slave looks like famine.
Sure he was got in a cheese-press, the whey runs out on's nose yet.
He will not yield above a peck of oysters
If I can get a quart of wine in too, you are gone, sir:
Why sure, thou hadst no father,

**1ST SLAVE**
Sure I know not.

**SLAVE-MERCHANT**
No, certainly; a March frog leap'd thy mother;
Thou'rt but a monster-paddock. Look who comes, sirrah.

[Exit **SERVANT**.

And next prepare the song, and do it lively.
Your tricks too, sirrah, they are ways to catch the buyer, [To the **ENGLISH SLAVE**]
And if you do them well, they'll prove good dowries.
How now?

[Re-enter **SERVANT**.

**SERVANT**
They come, sir, with their bags full loaden.

**SLAVE-MERCHANT**
Reach me my stool. O! here they come.

[Enter **PAULO**, **APOTHECARY**, **CUCULO**, and **CITIZENS**.

**CUCULO**
That's he.
He never fails monthly to sell his slaves here;
He buys them presently upon their taking,
And so disperses them to every market.

**SLAVE-MERCHANT**
Begin the song, and chant it merrily.

A SONG, by one of the **SLAVES**.

Well done.

**PAULO**
Good morrow!

**SLAVE-MERCHANT**
Morrow to you, signiors!

**PAULO**
We come to look upon your slaves, and buy too,
If we can like the persons, and the prices.

**CUCULO**
They shew fine active fellows.

**SLAVE-MERCHANT**
They are no less, sir,
And people of strong labours.

**PAULO**

That's in the proof, sir.

**APOTHECARY**
Pray what's the price of this red-bearded fellow?
If his gall be good, I have certain uses for him.

**SLAVE-MERCHANT**
My sorrel slaves are of a lower price,
Because the colour's faint: fifty chequins, sir.

**APOTHECARY**
What be his virtues?

**SLAVE-MERCHANT**
He will poison rats;
Make him but angry, and his eyes kill spiders;
Let him but, fasting, spit upon a toad,
And presently it bursts, and dies; his dreams kill:
He'll run you in a wheel, and draw up water,
But if his nose drop in't, 'twill kill an army.
When you have worn him to the bones with uses,
Thrust him into an oven luted well,
Dry him, and beat him, flesh and bone, to powder,
And that kills scabs, and aches of all climates.

**APOTHECARY**
Pray at what distance may I talk to him?

**SLAVE-MERCHANT**
Give him but sage and butter in a morning,
And there's no fear: but keep him from all women,
For there his poison swells most.

**APOTHECARY**
I will have him.
Cannot he breed a plague too?

**SLAVE-MERCHANT**
Yes, yes, yes,
Feed him with logs; pi-vvamm. Now to you, sir.
Do you like this slave?

[Pointing to **ANTONIO**.

**CUCULO**
Yes, if I like his price well.

**SLAVE-MERCHANT**

The price is full an hundred, nothing bated.
Sirrah, sell the Moors there: feel, he's high and lusty,
And of a gamesome nature; bold, and secret,
Apt to win favour of the man that owns him,
Offer to swear he has eaten nothing in a
By diligence and duty: look upon him.

**PAULO**
Do you hear, sir?

**SLAVE-MERCHANT**
I'll be with you presently—
Mark but his limbs, that slave will cost you four-score

[Pointing to the **CAPTAIN**.

**SLAVE-MERCHANT**
An easy price turn him about, and view him.
For these two, sir? why, they are the finest children
Twins, on my credit, sir. Do you see this boy, sir?
He will run as far from you in an hour—

**1ST CITIZEN**
Will he so, sir?

**SLAVE-MERCHANT**
Conceive me rightly, if upon an errand,
As any horse you have.

**2ND CITIZEN**
What will this girl do?

**SLAVE-MERCHANT**
Sure no harm at all, sir,
For she sleeps most an end.

**CITIZEN**
An excellent housewife.
Of what religion are they?

**SLAVE-MERCHANT**
What you will, sir,
So there be meat and drink in't: they'll do little
That shall offend you, for their chief desire
Is to do nothing at all, sir.

**CUCULO**
A hundred is too much.

**SLAVE-MERCHANT**
Not a doit bated:
He's a brave slave, his eye shews activeness;
Fire and the mettle of a man dwell in him.
Here is one you shall have

**CUCULO**
For what?

**SLAVE-MERCHANT**
For nothing,
And thank you too.

**PAULO**
What can he do?

**SLAVE-MERCHANT**
Why, anything that's ill,
And never blush at 'it: he's so true a thief,
That he'll steal from himself, and think he has got by it.
He stole out of his mother's belly, being an infant;
And from a lousy nurse he stole his nature,
From a dog his look, and from an ape his nimbleness;
He will look in your face and pick your pockets,
Rob ye the most wise rat of a cheese-paring;
There, where a cat will go in, he will follow,
His body has no backbone. Into my company

**CUCULO**
Come, follow me.

[Exit with **ANTONIO**.

**CITIZEN**
Twenty chequins for these two.

**SLAVE-MERCHANT**
For five and twenty take them.

**CITIZEN**
There's your money;
I'll have them, if it be to sing in cages.

**SLAVE-MERCHANT**
Give them hard eggs, you never had such blackbirds.

**CITIZEN**

Is she a maid, dost think?

**SLAVE-MERCHANT**
I dare not swear, sir:
She is nine year old, at ten you shall find few here.

**CITIZEN**
A merry fellow! thou say'st true.
Come, children.

[Exit with the **TWO MOORS**.

**PAULO**
Here, tell your money; if his life but answer
His outward promises, I have bought him cheap, sir.

**SLAVE-MERCHANT**
Too cheap, o' conscience: he's a pregnant knave;
Full of fine thought, I warrant him.

**PAULO**
He's but weak-timber'd.

**SLAVE-MERCHANT**
'Tis the better, sir;
He will turn gentleman a great deal sooner.

**PAULO**
Very weak legs.

**SLAVE-MERCHANT**
Strong, as the time allows, sir.

**PAULO**
What's that fellow?

**SLAVE-MERCHANT**
Who, this? the finest thing in all the world, sir,
The punctuallest, and the perfectest; an
English metal,
But coin'd in France: Your servant's servant, sir!
Do you understand that? or your shadow s servant!
Will you buy him to carry in a box? Kiss your hand, sirrah;—
Let fall your cloak on one shoulder; face to your left hand;
Feather your hat; slope your hat; now charge. Your honour,
What think you of this fellow?

**PAULO**

Indeed, I know not;
I never saw such an ape before: but, hark you,
Are these things serious in his nature?

**SLAVE-MERCHANT**
Yes, yes;
Part of his creed: come, do some more devices.
Quarrel a little, and take him for your enemy,
Do it in dumb show. Now observe him neai'ly.

[The **ENGLISH SLAVE** practises his posh

**PAULO**
This fellow's mad, stark mad.

**SLAVE-MERCHANT**
Believe they are all so:
I have sold a hundred of them.

**PAULO**
A strange nation!
What may the women be?

**SLAVE-MERCHANT**
As mad as they,
And, as I have heard for truth, a great deal madder:
Yet, you may find some civil things amongst them,
But they are not respected. Nay, never wonder;
They have a city, sir, I have been in
And therefore dare affirm it, where, if you saw
With what a load of vanity 'tis fraughted,
How like an everlasting morris-dance it looks,
Nething but hobby-horse, and maid Marianj
You would start indeed.

**PAULO**
They are handsome men?

**SLAVE-MERCHANT**
Yes, if they would thank their maker,
And seek no further; but they have new creators,
God-tailor, and god-mercer: a kind of Jews, sir,
But fall'n into idolatry; for they worship
Nothing with so much service, as the cow calves.

**PAULO**
What do you mean by cow-calves

**SLAVE-MERCHANT**
Why, their women.
Will you see him do any more tricks?

**PAULO**
'Tis enough, I thank you;
But yet I'll buy him, for the rareness of him
He may make my princely patient mirth and that done,
I'll chain him in my study, that at void hours
I may run o'er the story of his country.-

**SLAVE-MERCHANT**
His price is forty.

**PAULO**
Hold I'll once be foolish,
And buy a lump of levity to laugh at.

**APOTHECARY**
Will your worship walk?

**PAULO**
How now, apothecary,
Have you been buying too?

**APOTHECARY**
A little, sir,
A dose or two of mischief.

**PAULO**
Fare ye well, sir,
As these prove, we shall look the next wine for you.

**SLAVE-MERCHANT**
I shall be with you, sir.

**PAULO**
Who bought this fellow?

**2ND CITIZEN**
Not I.

**APOTHECARY**
Nor I.

**PAULO**
Why does he follow tis, then?

**SLAVE-MERCHANT**
Did not I tell you he would steal to you?

**2ND CITIZEN**
Sirrah,
You mouldy-chaps! know your crib, I would wish you,
And get from whence you came,

**1ST SLAVE**
I came from no place.

**PAULO**
Wilt thou be my fool? for fools, they say, will tell truth,

**1ST SLAVE**
Yes, if you will give me leave, sir, to abuse you,
For I can do that naturally.

**PAULO**
And I can beat you.

**1ST SLAVE**
I should be sorry else, sir.

**SLAVE-MERCHANT**
He looks for that, as duly as his victuals,
And will be extreme sick when he is not beaten.
He will be as wanton, when he has a bone broken,
As a cat in a bowl on the water.

**PAULO**
You will part with him?

**SLAVE-MERCHANT**
To such a friend as you, sir.

**PAULO**
And without money?

**SLAVE-MERCHANT**
Not a penny, signior;
And would he were better for you!

**PAULO**
Follow me, then;
The knave may teach me something.

**1ST SLAVE**

Something that
You dearly may repent; howe'er you scorn me,
The slave may prove your master.

**PAULO**
Farewell once more!

**SLAVE-MERCHANT**
Farewell! and when the wind serves next, expect me.

[Exeunt.


SCENE II. A Room in the Viceroy's Palace

Enter **CUCULO** and **ANTONIO**.

**CUCULO**
Come, sir, you are mine, sir, now; you serve a man, sir,
That, when you know more, you will find

**ANTONIO**
I hope so.

**CUCULO**
What dost thou hope?

**ANTONIO**
To find you a kind master.

**CUCULO**
Find you yourself a diligent true servant,
And take the precept of the wise before you,
And then you may hope, sirrah. Understand,
You serve me what is ME? a man of credit.

**ANTONIO**
Yes, sir.

**CUCULO**
Of special credit, special office; hear first
And understand again, of special office:
A man that nods upon the thing he meets,
And that thing bows.

**ANTONIO**
Tis fit it should be so, sir.

**CUCULO**

It shall be so: a man near all importance.
Dost thou digest this truly?

**ANTONIO**

I hope I shall, sir.

**CUCULO**

Besides, thou art to serve a noble mistress,
Of equal place and trust. Serve usefully,
Serve all with diligence, but her delights;
There make your stop. She is a woman, sirrah,
And though a cull'd out virtue, yet a woman.
Thou art not troubled with the strength of blood,
And stirring faculties, for she'll shew a fair one?

**ANTONIO**

As I am a man, I may; but as I am your man,
Your trusty, useful man, those thoughts shall perish.

**CUCULO**

'Tis apt, and well distinguish'd. The next precept,
And then, observe me, you have all your duty;
Keep, as thou'dst keep thine eye-sight, all wine from her,
All talk of wine.

**ANTONIO**

Wine is a comfort, sir.

**CUCULO**

A devil, sir! let her not dream of wine;
Make her believe there neither is, nor was wine;
Swear it.

**ANTONIO**

Will you have me lie?

**CUCULO**

To my end, sir:
For if one drop of wine but creep into her,
She is the wisest woman in the world straight,
And all the women in the world together
Are but a whisper to her; a thousand iron mills
Can be heard no further than a pair of nut-rackers.
Keep her from wine; wine makes her dangerous.
Fall back my lord Don Pedro!

[Enter **PEDRO**

**PEDRO**

Now, master Office,
What is the reason that your vigilant
Greatness, And your wife's wonderful
Wiseness, have lock'd up from me
The way to see my mistress?
Whose dog's dead now,
That you observe these vigils?

**CUCULO**

Very well, my lord.
Belike, we observe no law then, nor no order,
Nor feel no power, nor will, of him that made them,
When state-commands thus slightly are disputed.

**PEDRO**

What state command? dost thou think any state
Would give thee anything but eggs to keep,
Or trust thee with a' secret above lousing?

**CUCULO**

No, no, my lord, I am not passionate;
You cannot work me that way, to betray me.
A point there is in't, that you must not see, sir,
A secret and a serious point of state too;
And do not urge it further, do not, lord,
It will not take; you deal with them that wink not.
You tried my wife. Alas! you thought she was foolish,
Won with an empty word; you have not found it.

**PEDRO**

I have found a pair of coxcombs, that I am sure on.

**CUCULO**

Your lordship may say three: 1 ant not passionate.

**PEDRO**

How's that?

**CUCULO**

Your lordship found a faithful gentle-woman,
Strong, and inscrutable as the viceroy's heart;
A woman of another making, lord:
And, lest she might partake with woman's weakness,
I've purchased her a rib to make her perfect,
A rib that will not shrink, nor break in the bending.
This trouble we are put to, to prevent things,

Which your good lordship holds but necessary.

**PEDRO**
A fellow of a handsome and free promise,
And much, methinks, Tm taken with his countenance.
Do you serve this yeoman, porter?
[To **ANTONIO,**

**CUCULO**
Not a word.
Basta! Your lordship may discourse your freedom;
He is a slave of state, sir, so of silence.

**PEDRO**
You are very punctual, state-cut, fare ye well;
I shall find time to fit you too, I fear not.

[Exit.

**CUCULO**
And I shall fit you, lord: you would be billing;
You are too hot, sweet lord, too hot. Go you home,
And there observe these lessons I first taught you.
Look to your charge abundantly; be wary,
Trusty and wary; much weight hangs upon
Watchful and wary too! this lord is dangerous,
Take courage and resist: for other uses,
Your mistress will inform you. Go, be faithful,
And, do you hear? no wine.

**ANTONIO**
I shall observe, sir.

[Exeunt.

SCENE III. Another Room in the Same

Enter **PAULO** and **SURGEONS**.

**PAULO**
He must take air.

**1ST SURGEON**
Sir, under your correction,
The violence of motion may make
His wounds bleed fresh.

**2ND SURGEON**
And he hath lost already
Too much blood, in my judgment.

**PAULO**
I allow that;
But to choke up his spirits in a dark room,
Is far more dangerous. He comes; no questions.

[Enter **CARDENES**.

**CARDENES**
Certain we have no reason, nor that soul
Created of that pureness books persuade us:
We understand not, sure, nor feel that sweetness
That men call virtue's chain to link our actions.
Our imperfections form, and flatter us;
A will to rash and rude things is our reason,
And that we glory in, that makes us guilty.
Why did I wrong this man? unmanly wrong him?
Unmannerly? He gave me no occasion.
In all my heat how noble was his temper!
And, when I had forgot both man and manhood,
With what a gentle bravery did he chide me!
And, say he had kill'd me, whither had I travell'd?
Kill'd me in all my rage oh, how it shakes me!
Why didst thou do this, fool? a woman taught me,
The devil and his angel, woman, bade me.
I am a beast, the wildest of all beasts,
And like a beast I make my blood my master.
Farewell, farewell, forever, name of mistress!
Out of my heart I cross thee; love and women
Out of my thoughts.

**PAULO**
Ay, now you shew your manhood.

**CARDENES**
Doctor, believe me, I have bought my knowledge,
And dearly, doctor: they are dangerous creatures,
They sting at both ends, doctor; worthless creatures,
And all their loves and favours end in ruins.

**PAULO**
To man, indeed.

**CARDENES**

Why, now thou tak'st me rightly.
What can they shew, or by what act deserve us,
While we have Virtue, and pursue her beauties!

**PAULO**
And yet I've heard of many virtuous women.

**CARDENES**
Not many, doctor; there your reading fails you:
Would there were more, and in their loves less dangers!

**PAULO**
Love is a noble thing without all doubt, sir.

**CARDENES**
Yes, and an excellent to cure the itch.

[Exit.

**1ST SURGEON**
Strange melancholy!

**PAULO**
By degrees 'twill lessen:
Provide your things.

**2ND SURGEON**
Our care shall not be wanting.

[Exeunt.


SCENE IV. A Room in Cuculo's House

Enter **LEONORA** and **ALMIRA**.

**LEONORA**
Good madam, for your health's sake clear those clouds up,
That feed upon your beauties like diseases.
Time's hand will turn again, and what he ruins
Gently restore, and wipe off all your sorrows.
Believe you are to blame, much to blame, lady;
You tempt his loving care whose eye has number'd
All our afflictions, and the time to cure them:
You rather with this torrent choak his mercies,
Than gently slide into his providence.
Sorrows are well allow'd, and sweet nature,

Where they express no more than drops on lilies;
But, when they fall in storms, they bruise our hopes;
Make us unable, though our comforts meet us,
To hold our heads up: Come, you shall take comfort;
This is a sullen grief becomes condemn'd men,
That feel a weight of sorrow through their souls:
Do but look up. Why, so! is not this better,
Than hanging down your head still like a violet,
And dropping out those sweet eyes for a wager?
Pray you, speak a little.

**ALMIRA**
Pray you, desire no more;
And, if you love me, say no more.

**LEONORA**
How fain,
If I would be as wilful, and partake in't,
Would you destroy yourself! how often, lady,
Even of the same disease have you cured me,
And shook me out on't; chid me, tumbled me,
And forced my hands, thus?

**ALMIRA**
By these tears, no more.

**LEONORA**
You are too prodigal of them. Well,
I will not;
For though my love bids me transgress your will,
I have a service to your sorrows still.

[Exeunt.

SCENE V. A Hall in the Same

Enter **PEDRO** and **ANTONIO**.

**ANTONIO**
Indeed, my lord, my place is not so near:
I wait below stairs, and there sit, and wait
Who comes to seek accesses; nor is it fit, sir,
My rudeness should intrude so near their lodgings.

**PEDRO**
Thou mayst invent a way, 'tis but a trial,

But carrying up this letter, and this token,
And giving them discreetly to my mistress,
The lady Leonora: there's my purse,
Or anything thou'lt ask me; if thou knew'st me,
And what I may be to thee for this courtesy

**ANTONIO**
Your lordship speaks so honestly, and freely,
That by my troth I'll venture.

**PEDRO**
I dearly thank thee.

**ANTONIO**
And it shall cost me hard; nay, keep your purse, sir,
For, though my body's bought, my mind was never.
Though I am bound, my courtesies are no slaves.

**PEDRO**
Thou should'st be truly gentle.

**ANTONIO**
If I were so,
The state I am in bids you not believe it.
But to the purpose, sir; give me your letter,
And next your counsel, for I serve a crafty mistress.

**PEDRO**
And she must be removed, thou wilt else ne'er do it.

**ANTONIO**
Ay, there's the plague: think, and
I'll think awhile too.

**PEDRO**
Her husband's suddenly fallen sick?

**ANTONIO**
She cares not;
If he were dead, indeed, it would do better.

**PEDRO**
Would he were hang'd!

**ANTONIO**
Then she would run for joy, sir.

**PEDRO**

Some lady crying out?

**ANTONIO**
She has two already.

**PEDRO**
Her house afire?

**ANTONIO**
Let the fool, my husband, quench it.
This will be her answer. This may take; it will, sure.
Your lordship must go presently, and send me
Two or three bottles of your best Greek wine,
The strongest and the sweetest.

**PEDRO**
Instantly:
But will that do?

**ANTONIO**
Let me alone to work it.

[Exit **PEDRO**

Wine I was charged to keep by all means from her;
All secret locks it opens, and all counsels,
That I am sure, and gives men all accesses.
Pray heaven she be not loving when she's drunk now!
For drunk she shall be, though my pate pay for it.
She'll turn my stomach then abominably.
She has a most wicked face, and that lewd face
Being a drunken face, what face will there be!
She cannot ravish me. Now, if my master
Should take her so, and know I minister 'd,
What will his wisdom do? I hope be drunk too,
And then all's right. Well, lord, to do thee service
Above these puppet-plays, I keep a life ye:
Here come the executioners.

[Enter **SERVANT** with bottles.

You are welcome;
Give me your load, and tell my lord I am at it.

**SERVANT**
I will, sir; speed you, sir.

[Exit.

**ANTONIO**
Good speed on all sides!
'Tis strong, strong wine: O, the yaws that she will make!
Look to your stern, dear mistress, and steer right,
Here's that will work as high as the Bay of Portugal.
Stay, let me see I'll try her by the nose first;
For, if she be a right sow, sure she 'll find it.
She is yonder by herself, the ladies from her.
Now to begin my sacrifice:

[Pours out some of the wine.

—she stirs, and vents it.
O, how she holds her nose up like a jennet
In the wind of a grass mare! she has it full now,
And now she comes. I'll stand aside awhile.

[Enter **BORACHIA**.

**BORACHIA** [snuffing]
'Tis wine! ay, sure 'tis wine! excellent strong wine!
In the must, I take it: very wine! this way too.

**ANTONIO**
How true she hunts! I'll make the train a little longer.

[Pours out more wine.

**BORACHIA**
Stronger and stronger still! still! blessed wine!

**ANTONIO**
Now she hunts hot.

**BORACHIA**
All that I can for this wine!
This way it went, sure.

**ANTONIO**
Now she's at a cold scent.
Make out your doubles, mistress. O, well hunted!
That's she! that's she!

**BORACHIA**
O, if I could but see it!
Oh what a precious scent it has! but handle it!

**ANTONIO**
Now I'll untappice.

[Comes forward with the bottle.

**BORACHIA**
What's that? still 'tis stronger.
Why, how now, sirrah! what's that? Answer quickly,
And to the point.

**ANTONIO**
'Tis wine, forsooth, good wine,
Excellent Candy wine.

**BORACHIA**
'Tis well, forsooth!
Is this a drink for slaves? why, saucy sirrah,
(Excellent Candy wine!) draw nearer to me,
Reach me the bottle: why, thou most debauch'd slave:

**ANTONIO**
Pray be not angry, for with all my service
And pains, I purchased this for you, (I dare not drink it,)
For you a present; only for your pleasure;
To shew in little what a thanks I owe
The hourly courtesies your goodness gives me.

**BORACHIA**
And I will give thee more; there, kiss my hand on't.

**ANTONIO**
I thank you dearly for your dirty favour:
How rank it smells? [Aside.

**BORACHIA**
By thy leave, sweet bottle,
And sugar-candy wine, I now come to thee;
Hold your hand under.

**ANTONIO**
How does your worship like it?

**BORACHIA**
Under again again and now come kiss me;
I'll be a mother to thee: come, drink tome.

**ANTONIO**
I do beseech your pardon.

**BORACHIA**
Here's to thee, then;
I am easily entreated for thy good.
'Tis naught for thee, indeed; 'twill make thee break out;
Thou hast a pure complexion: now, for me
'Tis excellent, 'tis excellent for me.
Son slave, I've a cold stomach, and the wind

**ANTONIO**
Blows out a cry at both ends.

**BORACHIA**
Kiss again.
Cherish thy lips, for thou sh alt kiss fair ladies;
Son slave, I have them for thee; I'll shew thee all.

**ANTONIO**
Heaven bless mine eyes!

**BORACHIA**
Even all the secrets, son slave,
In my dominion.

**ANTONIO**
Oh! here come the ladies;
Now to my business.

[Enter **LEONORA** and **ALMIRA** behind.

**LEONORA**
This air will much refresh you.

**ALMIRA**
I must sit down.

**LEONORA**
Do, and take freer thoughts,
The place invites you; I'll walk by like your sentinel.

**BORACHIA**
And thou shalt be my heir, I'll leave thee all,
Heaven knows to what 'twill mount to; but abundance:
I'll leave thee two young ladies what think you of that, boy!

[**ANTONIO** goes to **LEONORA**.

Where is the bottle? two delicate young ladies:

But first you shall commit with me; do you mark, son?
And shew yourself a gentleman, that's the truth, son.

**ANTONIO**
Excellent lady, kissing your fair hand,
And humbly craving pardon for intruding,
This letter, and this ring

**LEONORA**
From whom, I pray you, sir?

**ANTONIO**
From the most noble, loving lord, don Pedro,
The servant of your virtues.

**BORACHIA**
And prithee, good son slave, be wise and circumspect,
And take heed of being o'ertaken with too much drink;
For it is a lamentable sin, and spoils all:
Why, 'tis the damnablest thing to be drunk, son!
Heaven can't endure it. And hark you, one thing I'd have done:
Knock my husband on the head, as soon as may be,
For he is an arrant puppy, and cannot perform
Why, where the devil is this foolish bottle?

**LEONORA**
I much thank you;
And this, sir, for your pains.

[Offers him her purse.

**ANTONIO**
No, gentle lady;
That I can do him service is my merit,
My faith, my full reward.

**LEONORA**
Once more, I thank you.
Since I have met so true a friend to goodness,
I dare deliver to your charge my answer:
Pray you, tell him, sir, this night I do invite him
To meet me in the garden; means he may find,
For love, they say, wants no abilities.

**ANTONIO**
Nor shall he, madam, if my help may prosper;
So everlasting love and sweetness bless you!
She's at it still, I dare not now appear to her.

**ALMIRA**
What fellow's that?

**LEONORA**
Indeed I know not, madam;
It seems of some strange country by his habit;
Nor can I shew you by what mystery
He wrought himself into this place, prohibited.

**ALMIRA**
A handsome man.

**LEONORA**
But of a mind more handsome.

**ALMIRA**
Was his business to you?

**LEONORA**
Yes, from a friend you wot of.

**ALMIRA**
A very handsome fellow,
And well demean'd.

**LEONORA**
Exceeding well; and speaks well.

**ALMIRA**
And speaks well, too?

**LEONORA**
Ay, passing well, and freely,
And, as he promises, of a most clear nature;
Brought up, sure, far above his shew.

**ALMIRA**
It seems so:
I would I'd heard him, friend. Comes he again?

**LEONORA**
Indeed I know not if he do.

**ALMIRA**
'Tis no matter.
Come, let's walk in.

**LEONORA**
I am glad you have found your tongue yet.

[Exeunt **LEONORA** and **ALMIRA**.

[**BORACHIA** sings.

**CUCULO** [within]
My wife is very merry; sure 'twas her voice:
Pray heaven there be no drink in't, then I allow it.

**ANTONIO**
Tis sure my master.

[Enter **CUCULO**.

Now the game begins;
Here will be spitting of fire o' both sides presently;
Send me but safe deliver'd!

**CUCULO**
O, my heart aches!
My head aches too: mercy o' me, she's perish'd!
She has gotten wine! she is gone for ever!

**BORACHIA**
Come hither, ladies, cany your bodies swimming;
Do your three duties, then then fall behind me.

**CUCULO**
O, thou pernicious rascal! what hast thou done?

**ANTONIO**
I done! alas, sir, I have done nothing.

**CUCULO**
Sirrah,
How came she by this wine?

**ANTONIO**
Alas, I know not.

**BORACHIA**
Who's that, that talks of wine there?

**ANTONIO**
Forsooth, my master.

**BORACHIA**
Bring him before me, son slave.

**CUCULO**
I will know it.
This bottle, how this bottle?

**BORACHIA**
Do not stir it;
For, if you do, by this good wine, I'll knock you,
I'll beat you damnably, yea and nay, I'll beat you;
And, when I have broke it 'bout your head, do you mark me?
Then will I tie it to your worship's tail,
And all the dogs in the town shall follow you.
No question, I would advise you, how I came by it;
I will have none of these points handled now.

**CUCULO**
She'll ne'er be well again while the world stands.

**ANTONIO** [Aside]
I hope so.

**CUCULO**
How dost thou, lamb?

**BORACHIA**
Well, God-a-mercy.
Belwether, how dost thou? Stand out, son slave,
Sit you here, and before this worshipful audience
Propound a doubtful question; see who's drunk now.

**CUCULO**
Now, now it works; the devil now dwells in her.

**BORACHIA**
Whether the heaven or the earth be nearer the moon?
Or what's the natural reason, why a woman longs
To make her husband cuckold? Bring me your cousin
The 'curate now, that great philosopher,
He that found out a pudding had two ends,
That learned clerk, that notable gymnosophist;
And let him with his Jacob's-staff discover
What is the third part of three farthings,
Three halfpence being the half, and I am satisfied.

**CUCULO**
You see she hath learning enough, if she could dispose it.

**BORACHIA**
Too much for thee, thou loggerhead, thou bull-head!

**CUCULO**
Nay, good Borachia.

**BORACHIA**
Thou a sufficient statesman!
A gentleman of learning! hang thee, dog-whelp;
Thou shadow of a man of action,
Thou scab o' the court! go sleep, you drunken rascal,
You debauch'd puppy; get you home, and sleep, sirrah;
And so will I: son slave, thou shalt sleep with me.

**CUCULO**
Prithee, look to her tenderly.

**BORACHIA**
No words, sirrah,
Of any wine, or anything like wine,
Or anything concerning wine, or by wine,
Or from, or with wine. Come, lead me like a countess.

**CUCULO**
Thus must we bear, poor men! there is a trick in't;
But, when she is well again, I'll trick her for it.

[Exeunt.

ACT IV

SCENE I. A Room in the Viceroy's Palace

Enter **PEDRO**.

**PEDRO**
Now, if this honest fellow do but prosper,
I hope I shall make fair return. I wonder
I hear not from the prince of Tarent yet,
I hope he's landed well, and to his safety;
The winds have stood most gently to his purpose.

[Enter **ANTONIO**.

My honest friend!

**ANTONIO**

Your lordship's poorest servant.

**PEDRO**

How hast thou sped?

**ANTONIO**

My lord, as well as wishes.
My way hath reach'd your mistress, and deliver 'd
Your love letter, and token; who, with all joy,
And virtuous constancy, desires to see you:
Commands you this night, by her loving power,
To meet her in the garden.

**PEDRO**

Thou hast made me;
I Redeem'd me, man, again from all my sorrows;
Done above wonder for me. Is it so?

**ANTONIO**

I should be now too old to learn to lie, sir,
And, as I live, I never was good flatterer.

**PEDRO**

I do see something in this fellow's face still,
That ties my heart fast to him. Let me love thee,
Nay, let me honour thee for this fair service:
And if I e'er forget it

**ANTONIO**

Good my lord,
The only knowledge of me is too much bounty:
My service, and my life, sir.

**PEDRO**

I shall think on't;
But how for me to get access?

**ANTONIO**

'Tis easy;
I'll be your guide, sir, all my care shall lead you;
My credit's better than you think.

**PEDRO**

I thank you,
And soon I'll wait your promise.

**ANTONIO**
With all my duty.

[Exeunt.


SCENE II. A Bedroom in the Same

Enter **VICEROY, DUKE of MESSINA, PAULO,** and **CUCULO.**

**PAULO**
All's as I tell you, princes; you shall here
Be witness to his fancies, melancholy
And strong imagination of his wrongs.
His inhumanity to don Antonio
Hath rent his mind into so many pieces
Of various imaginations, that,
Like the celestial bow, this colour now's
The object, then another, till all vanish.
He says a man might watch to death, or fast,
Or think his spirit out; to all which humours
I do apply myself, checking the bad,
And cherishing the good. For these, I have
Prepared my instruments, fitting his chamber
With trapdoors, and descents; sometimes presenting
Good spirits of the air, bad of the earth,
To pull down or advance his fair intentions.
He's of a noble nature, yet sometimes
Thinks that which, by confederacy, I do.
Is by some skill in magic.

[Enter **CARDENES**, a book in his hand.

Here he comes
Unsent. I do beseech you, what do you read, sir?

**CARDENES**
A strange position, which doth much perplex me:
That every soul's alike a musical instrument,
The faculties in all men equal strings,
Well or ill handled; and those sweet or harsh.

[Exit **PAULO.**

How like a fiddler I have play'd on mine then!
Declined the high pitch of my birth and breeding,
Like the most barbarous peasant; read my pride

Upon Antonio's meek humility,
Wherein he was far valianter than I.
Meekness, thou wait'st upon courageous spirits,
Enabling sufferance past inflictions.
In patience Tarent overcame me more
Than in my wounds: live then, no more to men,
Shut daylight from thine eyes, here cast thee down,

[Falls on the bed.

And with a sullen sigh breathe forth thy soul

[Re-enter **PAULO** disguised as a Friar.

What art? an apparition, or a man?

**PAULO**
A man, and sent to counsel thee.

**CARDENES**
Despair
Has stopt mine ears; thou seem'st a holy friar.

**PAULO**
I am; by doctor Paulo sent, to tell thee
Thou art too cruel to thyself, in seeking
To lend compassion and' aid to others.
My order bids me comfort thee. I have heard all
Thy various, troubled passions: hear but my story.
In way of youth I did enjoy one friend,
As good and perfect as heaven e'er made man;
This friend was plighted to a beauteous woman,
(Nature proud of her workmanship,) mutual love
Possess'd them both, her heart in his breast lodged,
And his in hers.

**CARDENES**
No more of love, good father,
It was my surfeit, and I loath it now,
As men in fevers meat they fell sick on.

**PAULO**
Howe'er, 'tis worth your hearing.
This betroth'd lady,
(The ties and duties of a friend forgotten,)
Spurr'd on by lust, I treacherously pursued;
Contemn 'd by her, and by my friend reproved,
Despised by honest men, my conscience sear'd up,

Love I converted into frantic rage;
And by that false guide led, I summon'd him
In this bad cause, his sword 'gainst mine, to prove
If he or I might claim most right in love.
But fortune, that does seld or never give
Success to right and virtue, made him fall
Under my sword. Blood, blood, a friend's dear blood,
A virtuous friend's, shed by a villain, me,
In such a monstrous and unequal cause,
Lies on my conscience.

**CARDENES**
And durst thou live,
After this, to be so old? 'tis an illusion
Raised up by charms: a man would not have lived.
Art quiet in thy bosom?

**PAULO**
As the sleep
Of infants.

**CARDENES**
My fault did not equal this;
Yet I have emptied my heart of joy,
Only to store sighs up. What were the arts
That made thee live so long in rest?

**PAULO**
Repentance
Hearty, that cleansed me; reason then confirm'd me,
I was forgiven, and took me to my beads.

[Exit.

**CARDENES**
I am in the wrong path; tender conscience
Makes me forget mine honour: I have done
No evil like this, yet I pine; whilst he,
A few tears of his true contrition tender 'd,
Securely sleeps. Ha! where keeps peace of conscience,
That I may buy her? nowhere; not in life.
'Tis feign'd that Jupiter two vessels placed,
The one with honey fill'd, the other gall,
At the entry of Olympus; Destiny,
There brewing these together, surfers not
One man to pass, before he drinks this mixture.
Hence it is we have not an hour of life
In which our pleasures relish not some pain,

Our sours some sweetness. Love doth taste of both;
Revenge, that thirsty dropsy of our souls,
Which makes us covet that which hurts us most,
Is not alone sweet, but partakes of tartness.

**DUKE of MESSINA**
Is't not a strange effect?

**VICEROY**
Past precedent.

**CUCULO**
His brain-pan's perish'd with his wounds: go to,
I knew 't would come to this.

**VICEROY**
Peace, man of wisdom.

**CARDENES**
Pleasure's the hook of evil; ease of care,
And so the general object of the court;
Yet some delights are lawful. Honour is
Virtue's allow'd ascent; honour, that clasps
All-perfect justice in her arms, that craves
No more respect than what she gives, that does
Nothing but what she'll suffer. This distracts me;
But I have found the right: had don Antonio
Done that to me, I did to him, I should have kill'd him;
The injury so foul, and done in public,
My footman would not bear it; then in honour
Wronging him so, I'll right him on myself:
There's honour, justice, and full satisfaction
Equally tender 'd; 'tis resolved, I'll do it.

[They rush forward and disarm him.

They take all weapons from me.

**DUKE of MESSINA**
Bless my son!

[Re-enter **PAULO**, dressed like a Soldier, and the **ENGLISH SLAVE** like a Courtier.

**VICEROY**
The careful doctor's come again.

**DUKE of MESSINA**
Rare man!

How shall I pay this debt?

**CUCULO**
He that is with him,
Is one o' the slaves he lately bought, he said,
To accommodate his cure: he's English born,
But French in his behaviour; a delicate slave.

**VICEROY**
The slave is very fine.

**CUCULO**
Your English slaves
Are ever so; I have seen an English slave
Far finer than his master: there's a state-point,
Worthy your observation.

**PAULO**
On thy life,
Be perfect in thy lesson: fewer legs, slave.

**CARDENES**
My thoughts are searchd and answer'd; for I did
Desire a soldier and a courtier,
To yield me satisfaction in some doubts
Not yet concluded of.

**PAULO**
Your doctor did
Admit us, sir.

**ENGLISH SLAVE**
And we are at your service;
Whate'er it be, command it.

**CARDENES**
You appear
A courtier in the race of LOVE; how far
In honour are you bound to run?

**ENGLISH SLAVE**
I'll tell you,
You must not spare expense, but wear gay clothes,
And you may be, too, prodigal of oaths,
To win a mistress' favour; not afraid
To pass unto her through her chambermaid.
You may present her gifts, and of all sorts,
Feast, dance, and revel; they are lawful sports:

The choice of suitors you must not deny her,
Nor quarrel, though you find a rival by her:
Build on your own deserts, and ever be
A strange'r to love's enemy, jealousy,
For that draws on

**CARDENES**
No more; this points at me;

[Exit **ENGLISH SLAVE**.

I ne'er observed these rules. Now speak, old soldier,
The height of HONOUR?

**PAULO**
No man to offend,
Ne'er to reveal the secrets of a friend;
Rather to suffer than to do a wrong;
To make the heart no stranger to the tongue;
Pro voiced, not to betray an enemy,
Nor eat his meat I choak with flattery;
Blushless to tell wherefore I wear my scars,
Or for my conscience, or my country's wars;
To aim at just things; if we have wildly run
Into offences, wish them all undone:
'Tis poor, in grief for a wrong done, to die,
Honour, to dare to live, and satisfy.

**VICEROY**
Mark, how he winds him.

**DUKE of MESSINA**
Excellent man!

**PAULO**
Who fights
With passions, and o'ercomes them, is endued
With the best virtue, passive fortitude.

[Exit.

**CARDENES**
Thou hast touch'd me, soldier; oh! this honour bears
The right stamp; would all soldiers did profess
Thy good religion! The discords of my soul
Are tuned, and make a heavenly harmony:
What sweet peace feel I now! I am ravish'd with it.

**VICEROY**
How still he sits!

[Music.

**CUCULO**
Hark! music.

**DUKE of MESSINA**
How divinely
This artist gathers scatter'd sense; with cunning
Composing the fair jewel of his mind,
Broken in pieces, and nigh lost before.

[Re-enter **PAULO**, dressed like a Philosopher, accompanied by a **GOOD** and **EVIL GENIUS**, who sing a song in alternate stanzas: during the performance of which Paulo goes off, and returns in his own shape.

**VICEROY**
See Protean Paulo in another shape.

**PAULO**
Away, I'll bring him shortly perfect, doubt not.

**DUKE of MESSINA**
Master of thy great art!

**VICEROY**
As such we'll hold thee.

**DUKE of MESSINA**
And study honours for him.

**CUCULO**
I'll be sick
On purpose to take physic of this doctor.

[Exeunt all but **CARDENES** and **PAULO**.

**CARDENES**
Doctor, thou hast perfected a body's cure
To amaze the world, and almost cured a mind
Near frenzy. With delight I now perceive,
You, for my recreation, have invented
The several objects, which my melancholy
Sometimes did think you conjured, other-whiles
Imagined them chimaeras. You have been
My friar, soldier, philosopher,
My poet, architect, physician;

Labour'd for me, more than your slaves for you,
In their assistance: in your moral song
Of my good Genius and my bad, you have won me
A cheerful heart, and banish'd discontent;
There being nothing wanting to my wishes,
But once more, were it possible, to behold
Don John Antonio.

**PAULO**
There shall be letters sent
Into all parts of Christendom, to inform him
Of your recovery, which now, sir, I doubt not.

**CARDENES**
What honours, what rewards can I heap on you!

**PAULO**
That my endeavours have so well succeeded,
Is a sufficient recompense. Pray you retire, sir;
Not too much air so soon.

**CARDENES**
I am obedient.

[Exeunt.


SCENE III. A Room in Cuculo's House

Enter **ALMIRA** and **LEONORA**.

**LEONORA**
How strangely
This fellow runs in her mind! [Aside.

**ALMIRA**
Do you hear, cousin?

**LEONORA**
Her sadness clean forsaken!

**ALMIRA**
A poor slave
I Bought for my governess, say you?

**LEONORA**
I hear so.

**ALMIRA**
And, do you think, a Turk?

**LEONORA**
His habit shows it;
At least bought for a Turk.

**ALMIRA**
Ay, that may be so.

**LEONORA**
What if he were one naturally?

**ALMIRA**
Nay, 'tis nothing,
Nothing to the purpose; and yet, methinks, 'tis strange
Such handsomeness of mind, and civil outside,
Should spring from those rude countries.

**LEONORA**
If it be no more,
I'll call our governess, and she can shew you.

**ALMIRA**
Why, do you think it is?

**LEONORA**
I do not think so.

**ALMIRA**
Fie! no, no, by no means; and to tell thee truth, wench,
I am truly glad he is here, be what he will:
Let him be still the same he makes a shew of;
For now we shall see something to delight us.

**LEONORA**
And heaven knows, we have need on't.

**ALMIRA**
Heigh ho! my heart aches.
Prithee, call in our governess.

[Exit **LEONORA**.

Plague o' this fellow!
Why do I think so much of him? how the devil
Creep'd he into my head? and yet, beshrew me,

Methinks I have not seen I lie, I have seen
A thousand handsomer, a thousand sweeter.
But say this fellow were adorn'd as they are,
Set off to shew and glory! What's that to me?
Fie, what a fool am I! what idle fancies
Buz in my brains!

[Re-enter **LEONORA** with **BORACHIA**.

**BORACHIA**
And how doth my sweet lady?
**LEONORA**
She wants your company to make her merry.

**BORACHIA**
And how does master Pug, I pray you, madam?

**LEONORA**
Do you mean her little dog?

**BORACHIA**
I mean his worship.

**LEONORA**
Troubled with fleas a little.

**BORACHIA**
Alas, poor chicken!

**LEONORA**
She's here, and drunk, very fine drunk, I take it;
I found her with a bottle for her bolster,
Lying along, and making love.

**ALMIRA**
Borachia,
Why, where hast thou been, wench? She looks not well, friend.
Art not with child?

**BORACHIA**
I promise ye, I know not;
I am sure my belly's full, and that's a shrewd sign:
Besides I am shrewdly troubled with a tiego
Here in my head, madam; often with this tiego,
It takes me very often.

**LEONORA**
I believe thee.

**ALMIRA**
You must drink wine.

**BORACHIA**
A little would do no harm, sure.

**LEONORA**
'Tis a raw humour blows into your head;
Which good strong wine will temper.

**BORACHIA**
I thank your highness.
I will be ruled, though much against my nature;
For wine I ever hated from my cradle:
Yet, for my good—

**LEONORA**
Ay, for your good, by all means.

**ALMIRA**
Borachia, what new fellow's that thou hast gotten?
(Now she will sure be free) that handsome stranger?

**BORACHIA**
How much wine must I drink, an't please your ladyship?

**ALMIRA**
She's finely greased! Why, two or three round draughts, wench.

**BORACHIA**
Fasting?

**ALMIRA**
At any time.

**BORACHIA**
I shall hardly do it:
But yet I'll try, good madam.

**LEONORA**
Do; 'twill work well.

**ALMIRA**
But, prithee answer me, what is this fellow?

**BORACHIA**
I'll tell you two: but let it go no further.

**LEONORA**
No, no, by no means.

**BORACHIA**
May I not drink before bed too?

**LEONORA**
At any hour.

**BORACHIA**
And say in the night it take me?

**ALMIRA**
Drink then: but what's this man?

**BORACHIA**
I'll tell ye, madam,
But pray you be secret; he's the great Turk's son, for certain,
And a fine Christian; my husband bought him for me:
He's circumsinged.

**LEONORA**
He's circumcised, thou wouldst say.

**ALMIRA**
How dost thou know?

**BORACHIA**
I had an eye upon him:
But even as sweet a Turk, an't like your ladyship,
And speaks ye as pure pagan: I'll assure ye,
My husband had a notable pennyworth of him;
And found me but the Turk's own son, his own son
By father and mother, madam!

**LEONORA**
She's mad-drunk.

**ALMIRA**
Prithee, Borachia, call him; I would see him,
And tell thee how I like him.

**BORACHIA**
As fine a Turk, madam,
For that which appertains to a true Turk

**ALMIRA**

Prithee, call him.

**BORACHIA**
He waits here at the stairs: Son slave! come hither.

[Enter **ANTONIO**.

Pray you give me leave a little to instruct him,
He's 'raw yet in the way of entertainment.
Son slave, where's the other bottle?

**ANTONIO**
In the bedstraw;
I hid it there.

**BORACHIA**
Go up, and make your honours.
Madam, the tiego takes me now, now, madam;
I must needs be unmannerly.

**ALMIRA**
Pray you be so.

**LEONORA**
You know your cure.

**BORACHIA**
In the bedstraw?

**ANTONIO**
There you'll find it.

[Exit **BORACHIA**.

**ALMIRA**
Come hither, sir: how long have you served here?

**ANTONIO**
A poor time, madam, yet, to shew my service.

**ALMIRA**
I see thou art diligent.

**ANTONIO**
I would be, madam;
Tis all the portion left me, that and truth.

**ALMIRA**

Thou art but young.

**ANTONIO**
Had fortune meant me so,
Excellent lady, time had not much wrong'd me.

**ALMIRA**
Wilt thou serve me?

**ANTONIO**
In all my prayers, madam,
Else such a misery as mine but blasts you.

**ALMIRA**
Beshrew my heart, he speaks well;
wondrous honestly. [Aside.

**ANTONIO**
Madam, your loving lord stays for you.

**LEONORA**
I thank you.
Your pardon for an hour, dear friend.

**ALMIRA**
Your pleasure.

**LEONORA**
I dearly thank you, sir.

[Exit.

**ANTONIO**
My humblest service.
She views me narrowly, yet sure she knows me not:
I dare not trust the time yet, nor I must not. [Aside.

**ALMIRA**
You are not as your habit shews?

**ANTONIO**
No, madam,
His hand, that, for my sins, lies heavy on me,
I hope will keep me from being a slave to the devil.

**ALMIRA**
A brave clear mind he has, and nobly season'd.
What country are you of?

**ANTONIO**
A Biscan, lady.

**ALMIRA**
No doubt, a gentleman,

**ANTONIO**
My father thought so.
Aim, Ay, and I warrant thee, a right fair woman
Thy mother was: he blushes, that confirms it.
Upon my soul, I have not seen such sweetness!
I prithee, blush again.

**ANTONIO**
'Tis a weakness, madam,
I am easily this way woo'd to.

**ALMIRA**
I thank you.
Of all that e'er I saw, thou art the perfectest. [Aside.
Now you must tell me, sir, for now I long for't.

**ANTONIO**
What would she have?

**ALMIRA**
The story of your fortune,
The hard and cruel fortune brought you hither.

**ANTONIO**
That makes me stagger; yet I hope
I'm hid still. [Aside.
That I came hither, madam, was the fairest.

**ALMIRA**
But how this misery you bear, fell on you?

**ANTONIO**
Infandum, regina, jubes renovare dolorem.

**ALMIRA**
Come, I will have it; I command you, tell it,
For such a speaker I would hear for ever.

**ANTONIO**
Sure, madam, 'twill but make you sad and heavy,

Because I know your goodness full of pity;
And 'tis so poor a subject too, and to your ears,
That are acquainted with things sweet and easy,
So harsh a harmony.

**ALMIRA**
I prithee speak it.

**ANTONIO**
I ever knew obedience the best sacrifice.
Honour of ladies, then, first passing over
Some few years of my youth, that are impertinent,
Let me begin the sadness of my story,
Where I began to lose myself, to love first.

**ALMIRA**
'Tis well, go forward; some rare piece I look for.

**ANTONIO**
Not far from where my father lives, a lady,
A neighbour by, bless'd with as great a beauty
As nature durst bestow without undoing,
Dwelt, and most happily, as I thought then,
And bless'd the house a thousand times she dwelt in.
This beauty, in the blossom of my youth,
When my first fire knew no adulterate incense,
Nor I no way to flatter, but my fondness;
In all the bravery my friends could shew me,
In all the faith my innocence could give me,
In the best language my true tongue could tell me,
And all the broken sighs my sick heart lend me,
I sued, and serv'd: long did I love this lady,
Long was my travail, long my trade to win her;
With all the duty of my soul I served her.

**ALMIRA**
How feelingly he speaks! [Aside]
And she loved you too?
It must be so.

**ANTONIO**
I would it had, dear lady;
This story had been needless, and this place,
I think, unknown to me.

**ALMIRA**
Were your bloods equal?

**ANTONIO**
Yes, and I thought our hearts too.

**ALMIRA**
Then she must love.

**ANTONIO**
She did but never me; she could not love me,
She would not love, she hated: more, she scorn'd me,
And in so poor and base a way abused me,
For all my services, for all my bounties,
So bold neglects flung on me.

**ALMIRA**
An ill woman!
Be like you found some rival in your love, then?

**ANTONIO**
How perfectly she points me to my story! [Aside.
Madam, I did; and one whose pride and anger,
Ill manners, and worse mien, she doted on,
Doted to my undoing, and my ruin.
And, but for honour to your sacred beauty,
And reverence to the noble sex, though she fall,
As she must fall that durst be so unnoble,
I should say something unbeseeming me.
What out of love, and worthy love, I gave her,
Shame to her most unworthy mind! to fools,
To girls, and fiddlers, to her boys she flung,
And in disdain of me.

**ALMIRA**
Pray you take me with you.
Of what complexion was she?

**ANTONIO**
But that I dare not
Commit so great a sacrilege gainst virtue,
She look'd not much unlikt though far, far short.
Something, I see, appears your pardon, madam
Her eyes would smile so, but her eyes would cozen;
And so she would look sad: but yours is pity,
A noble chorus to my wretched story;
Hers was disdain and cruelty.

**ALMIRA**
Pray heaven,
Mine be no worse! he has told me a strange story, [Aside.

And said 't would make me sad! he is no liar.
But where begins this poor state? I will have all,
For it concerns me truly.

**ANTONIO**
Last, to blot me
From all remembrance what I had been to her,
And how, how honestly, how nobly served her,
'Twas thought she set her gallant to dispatch me.
'Tis true, he quarrell'd without place or reason:
We fought, I kill'd him; heaven's strong hand was with me.
For which I lost my country, friends, acquaintance,
And put myself to sea, where a pirate took me,
Forcing this habit of a Turk upon me,
And sold me here.

**ALMIRA**
Stop there awhile; but stay still.

[Waits aside.

In this man's story, how I look, how monstrous!
How poor and naked now I shew! what don John,
In all the virtue of his life, but aim'd at,
This thing hath conquer'd with a tale, and carried.
Forgive me, thou that guid'st me! never conscience
Touch 'd me till now, nor true love: let me keep it.

[Re-enter **LEONORA** with **PEDRO**.

**LEONORA**
She is there. Speak to her, you will find her alter' d.

**PEDRO**
Sister, I am glad to see you, but far gladder,
To see you entertain your health so well.

**ALMIRA**
I am glad to see you too, sir, and shall be gladder
Shortly to see you all.

**PEDRO**
Now she speaks heartily.
What do you want?

**ALMIRA**
Only an hour of privateness;
I have a few thoughts

**PEDRO**
Take your full contentment,
We'll walk aside again; but first to you, friend,
Or I shall much forget myself: my best friend,
Command me ever, ever you have won it.

**ANTONIO**
Your lordship overflows me.

**LEONORA**
'Tis but due, sir,

[Exeunt **LEONORA** and **PEDRO**.

**ALMIRA**
He's there still. Come, sir, to your last part now,
Which only is your name, and I dismiss you.
Why, whither go you?

**ANTONIO**
Give me leave, good madam,
Or I must be so seeming rude to take it.

**ALMIRA**
You shall not go, I swear you shall not go:
I ask you nothing but your name; you have one,
And why should that thus fright you?

**ANTONIO**
Gentle madam,
I cannot speak; pray pardon me, a sickness,
That takes me often, ties my tongue: go from me,
My fit's infectious, lady.

**ALMIRA**
Were it death
In all his horrors, I must ask and know it;
Your sickness is unwillingness. Hard heart,
To let a lady of my youth, and place,
Beg thus long for a trifle!

**ANTONIO**
Worthiest lady,
Be wise, and let me go; you'll bless me for it,
Beg not that poison from me that will kill you.

**ALMIRA**

I only beg your name, sir.

**ANTONIO**
That will choak you;
I do beseech you, pardon me.

**ALMIRA**
I will not.

**ANTONIO**
You'll curse me when you hear it.

**ALMIRA**
Rather kiss thee;
Why shouldst thou think so?

**ANTONIO**
Why! I bear that name,
And most unluckily as now it happens,
(Though I be innocent of all occasion,)
That, since my coming hither, people tell me
You hate beyond forgiveness: now, heaven knows
So much respect, although I am a stranger,
Duty, and humble zeal, I bear your sweetness,
That for the world I would not grieve your goodness:
I'll change my name, dear madam.

**ALMIRA**
People lie,
And wrong thy name; thy name may save all others,
And make that holy to me, that I hated:
Prithee, what is't?

**ANTONIO**
Don John Antonio.
What will this woman do, what thousand changes
Run through her heart and hands? no fix'd thought in her!
She loves for certain now, but now I dare not.
Heaven guide me right! [Aside.

**ALMIRA**
I am not angry, sir,
With you, nor with your name; I love it rather,
And shall respect you you deserve for this time
I license you to go: be not far from me,)
I shall call for you often.

**ANTONIO**

I shall wait, madam.

[Exit.

[Enter **CUCULO**.

**ALMIRA**
Now, what's the news with you?

**CUCULO**
My lord your father
Sent me to tell your honour, prince Martino
Is well recovered, and in strength.

**ALMIRA**
Why, let him.
The stories and the names so well agreeing,
And both so noble gentlemen. [Aside.

**CUCULO**
And more, an't please you

**ALMIRA**
It doth not please me, neither more nor less on't.

**CUCULO**
They'll come to visit you.

**ALMIRA**
They shall break through the doors then.

[Exit.

**CUCULO**
Here's a new trick of state; this shews foul weather;
But let her make it when she please, I'll gain by it.

[Exit.


ACT V

SCENE I. A Street

Enter **PIRATES**, and the **SLAVE** that folio-died **PAULO**.

**1ST PIRATE**

Sold for a slave, say'st thou?

**SLAVE**
Twas not so well:
Though I am bad enough, I personated
Such base behaviour, barbarism of manners,
With other pranks that might deter the buyer,
That the market yielded not one man that would
Vouchsafe to own me.

**1ST PIRATE**
What was thy end in it?

**SLAVE**
To be given away for nothing, as I was
To the viceroy's doctor; with him I have continued
In such contempt, a slave unto his slaves;
His horse and dog of more esteem: and from
That villainous carriage of myself, as if
I'd been a lump of flesh without a soul,
I drew such scorn upon me, that I pass'd,
And pried in everyplace, without observance.
For which, if you desire to be made men,
And by one undertaking, and that easy,
You are bound to sacrifice unto my sufferings,
The seed I sow'd, and from which you shall reap
A plentiful harvest.

**1ST PIRATE**
To the point; I like not
These castles built in the air.

**SLAVE**
I'll make them real,
And you the Neptunes of the sea; you shall
No more be sea-rats.

**1ST PIRATE**
Art not mad?

**SLAVE**
You have seen
The star of Sicily, the fair Almira,
The viceroy's daughter, and the beauteous ward
Of the duke of Messina?

**1ST PIRATE**
Madam Leonora.

**SLAVE**
What will you say, if both these princesses,
This very night, for I will not delay you,
Be put in your possession?

**1ST PIRATE**
Now I dare swear
Thou hast maggots in thy brains, thou wouldst not else,
Talk of impossibilities.

**SLAVE**
Be still
Incredulous.

**1ST PIRATE**
Why, canst thou think we are able
To force the court?

**SLAVE**
Are we able to force two women,
And a poor Turkish slave? Where lies your pinnace?

**1ST PIRATE**
In a creek not half a league hence.

**SLAVE**
Can you fetch ladders,
To mount a garden wall?

**2ND PIRATE**
They shall be ready.

**SLAVE**
No more words then, but follow me; and if
I do not make this good, let my throat pay for't.

**1ST PIRATE**
What heaps of gold these beauties would bring to us
From the great Turk, if it were possible
That this could be effected!

**SLAVE**
If it be not,
I know the price on't.

**1ST PIRATE**
And be sure to pay it.

[Exeunt.


SCENE II. A Room in Cuculo's House

Enter **ANTONIO** with a letter in his hand.

**ANTONIO**
Her fair hand threw this from the window to me,
And as I took it up, she said, Peruse it,
And entertain a fortune offer d to thee.
What may the inside speak?

[Breaks it open, and reads.

For satisfaction
Of the contempt I shew' d don John Antonio,
Whose name thou bear'st, and in that dearer to me,
I do profess I love thee How! tis so
I love thee; this night wait me in the garden.
There thou shalt know more subscribed,
Thy Almira.
Can it be possible such levity
Should wait on her perfections! when I was
Myself, set off with all the grace of greatness,
Pomp, bravery, circumstance, she hated me,
And did profess it openly; yet now,
Being a slave, a thing she should in reason
Disdain to look upon; in this base shape,
And, since I wore it, never did her service,
To dote thus fondly! and yet I should glory
In her revolt from constancy, not accuse it,
Since it makes for me. But, ere I go further,
Or make discovery of myself, I'll put her
To the utmost trial. In the garden! well,
There I shall learn more. Women, giddy women!
In her the blemish of your sex you prove,
There is no reason for your hate or love.

[Exit.


SCENE III. A Garden Belonging to the Same

Enter **ALMIRA, LEONORA,** and **TWO WAITING-WOMEN.**

**LEONORA**
At this
Unseasonable time to be thus brave,
No visitants expected! you amaze me.

**ALMIRA**
Are these jewels set forth to the best advantage,
To take the eye?

**1ST WAITING-WOMAN**
With our best care.

**2ND WAITING-WOMAN**
We never
Better discharged our duties.

**ALMIRA**
In my sorrows,
A princess' name (I could perceive it) struck
A kind of reverence in him, and my beauty,
As then neglected, forcèd him to look on me
With some sparks of affection; but now,
When I would fan them to a glorious flame,
I cannot be too curious. I wonder
He stays so long. [Aside.

**LEONORA**
These are strange fancies.

**ALMIRA**
Go,
Entreat I do forget myself command
My governess' gentleman her slave, I should say,
To wait me instantly;

[Exit **WAITING-WOMEN**.

—and yet already
He's here; his figure graven on my heart,
Never to be razed out.

[Enter **PIRATES**, and the **SLAVE**.

**SLAVE**
There is the prize.
Is it so rich that you dare not seize upon it?
Here I begin.

[Seizes **ALMIRA**.

**ALMIRA**
Help! villain!

**1ST PIRATE**
You are mine.

[Seizes **LEONORA**.

**2ND PIRATE**
Though somewhat coarse, you'll serve, after a storm,
To bid fair weather welcome.

[Seizes **2ND WAITING-WOMAN**.

**LEONORA**
Ravisher!
Defend me, heaven!

**ALMIRA**
No aid near!

**2ND WAITING-WOMAN**
Help!

**SLAVE**
Dispatch.
No glove nor handkerchief to stop their mouths?
Their cries will reach the guard, and then we are lost.

[Re-enter **1ST WAITING-WOMAN**, with **ANTONIO**.

**ANTONIO**
What shrieks are these? from whence? O blessed saints,
What sacrilege to beauty! do I talk,
When 'tis almost too late to do!

[Forces a sword from the **SLAVE**.

Take that.

**SLAVE**
All set upon him.

**1ST PIRATE**
Kill him.

**ANTONIO**
You shall buy
My life at a dear rate, you rogues.

[Enter **PEDRO**, **CUCULO**, **BORACHIA**, and **GUARD**.

**CUCULO**
Down with them!

**PEDRO**
Unheard-of treason!

**BORACHIA**
Make in, loggerhead;
My son slave fights like a dragron: take my bottle,
Drink courage out on't.

**ANTONIO**
Madam, you are free.

**PEDRO**
Take comfort, dearest mistress.

**CUCULO**
O you micher,
Have you a hand in this?

**SLAVE**
My aims were high;
Fortune's my enemy, to die's the worst,
And that I look for.

**1ST PIRATE**
Vengeance on your plots!

**PEDRO**
The rack at better leisure shall force from them
A full discovery: away with them.

**CUCULO**
Load them with irons.

**BORACHIA**
Let them have no wine

[Exit **GUARD** with **PIRATES** and **SLAVE**.

To comfort their cold hearts.

**PEDRO**
Thou man of men!

**LEONORA**
A second Hercules.

**ALMIRA**
An angel thus disguised.

**PEDRO**
What thanks?

**LEONORA**
What service?

**BORACHIA**
He shall serve me, by your leave, no service else.

**ANTONIO**
I have done nothing but my duty, madam;
And if the little you have seen exceed it,
The thanks due for it pay my watchful master,
And this my sober mistress.

**BORACHIA**
He speaks truth, madam,
I am very sober.

**PEDRO**
Far beyond thy hopes
Expect reward.

**ALMIRA**
We'll straight to court, and there
It is resolved what I will say and do.
I am faint, support me.

**PEDRO**
This strange accident
Will be heard with astonishment. Come, friend,
You have made yourself a fortune, and deserve it.

[Exeunt.

SCENE IV. A Room in the Viceroy's Palace

Enter **VICEROY**, **DUKE of MESSINA**, and **PAULO**.

**DUKE of MESSINA**
Perfectly cured!

**PAULO**
As such I will present him:
The thanks be given to heaven.

**DUKE of MESSINA**
Thrice-reverend man,
What thanks but will come short of thy desert?
Or bounty, though all we possess were given thee,
Can pay thy merit? I will have thy statue
Set up in brass.

**VICEROY**
Thy name made the sweet subject
Of our best poems; thy unequall'd cures
Recorded to posterity.

**PAULO**
Such false glories
(Though the desire of fame be the last weakness
Wise men put off) are not the marks I shoot at:
But, if I have done anything that may challenge
Your favours, mighty princes, my request is,
That for the good of such as shall succeed me,
A college for physicians may be
With care and cost erected, in which no man
May be admitted to a fellowship,
By such as by their vigilant studies shall
Deserve a place there; this magnificence,
Posterity shall thank you for.

**VICEROY**
Rest assured,
In this, or any boon you please to ask,
You shall have no repulse.

**PAULO**
My humblest service
Shall ne'er be wanting. Now, if you so please,
I'll fetch my princely patient, and present him.

**DUKE of MESSINA**

Do; and imagine in what I may serve you,
And, by my honour, with a willing hand
I will subscribe to't.

[Exit **PAULO**.

[Enter **PEDRO**, **ALMIRA**, **LEONORA**, **ANTONIO**, **CUCULO**, **BORACHIA**, and **GUARD**.

**CUCULO**
Make way there.

**VICEROY**
My daughter!
How's this! a slave crown'd with a civic garland!
The mystery of this?

**PEDRO**
It will deserve
Your hearing and attention: such a truth
Needs not rhetorical flourishes, and therefore
With all the brevity and plainness that
I can, I will deliver it. If the old Romans,
When of most power and wisdom, did decree
A wreath like this to any common soldier
That saved a citizen's life, the bravery
And valour of this man may justly challenge
Triumphant laurel. This last night a crew
Of pirates brake in signior Cuculo's house,
With violent rudeness seizing on my sister,
And my fair mistress; both were in their power,
And ready to be forced hence, when this man,
Unarm'd, came to their rescue, but his courage
Soon furnish'd him with weapons; in a word,
The lives and liberties of these sweet ladies,
You owe him for: the rovers are in hold,
And ready, when you please, for punishment.

**VICEROY**
As an induction of more to come,
Receive this favour.

**DUKE of MESSINA**
With myself, my son
Shall pay his real thanks. He comes; observe now
Their amorous meeting.

[Re-enter **PAULO** with **CARDENES**.

**CARDENES**
I am glad you are well, lady.

**ALMIRA**
I grieve not your recovery.

**VICEROY**
So coldly!

**DUKE of MESSINA**
Why fall you off?

**CARDENES**
To shun captivity, sir.
I was too long a slave, I'll now be free.

**ALMIRA**
'Tis my desire you should. Sir, my affection
To him was but a trifle, which I play'd with
In the childhood of my love; which now, grown older,
I cannot like of.

**VICEROY**
Strange inconstancy!

**CARDENES**
'Tis judgment, sir, in me, or a true debt
Tender 'd to justice, rather. My first life,
Loaden with all the follies of a man,
Or what could take addition from a woman,
Was by my headstrong passions, which o'er
My understanding, forfeited to death:
But this new being, this my second life,
Begun in serious contemplation of
What best becomes a perfect man, shall never
Sink under such weak frailties.

**DUKE of MESSINA**
Most unlook'd for!

**PAULO**
It does transcend all wonders.

**CARDENES**
'Tis a blessing
I owe your wisdom, which I'll not abuse:
But if you envy your own gift, and will
Make me that wretched creature which I was,

You then again shall see me passionate,
A lover of poor trifles, confident
In man's deceiving strength, or falser fortune;
Jealous, revengeful, in unjust things daring,
Injurious, quarrelsome, stored with all diseases
The beastly part of man infects his soul with,
And to remember what's the worst, once more
To love a woman; but till that time never.

[Exit.

**VICEROY**
Stand you affected so to men,
Almira?

**ALMIRA**
No, sir; if so, I could not well discharge
What I stand bound to pay you, and to nature.
Though prince Martino does profess a hate
To womankind, 'twere a poor world for women,
Were there no other choice, or all should follow
The example of this new Hippolytus:
There are men, sir, that can love, and have loved truly;
Nor am! desperate but I may deserve
One that both can and will so.

**VICEROY**
My allowance
Shall rank with your good liking, still provided
Your choice be worthy.

**ALMIRA**
In it I have used
The judgment of my mind, and that made clearer
With calling oft to heaven it might be so.
I have not sought a living comfort from
The reverend ashes of old ancestors;
Nor given myself to the mere name and titles
Of such a man, that, being himself nothing,
Derives his substance from his grandsire's tomb:
For wealth, it is beneath my birth to think on't,
Since that must wait upon me, being your daughter;
No, sir, the man I love, though he wants all
The setting forth of fortune, gloss and greatness,
Has in himself such true and real goodness,
His parts so far above his low condition,
That he will prove an ornament, not a blemish,
Both to your name and family.

**PEDRO**
What strange creature
Hath she found out?

**LEONORA**
I dare not guess.

**ALMIRA**
To hold you
No longer in suspense, this matchless man,
That saved my life and honour, is my husband,
Whom I will serve with duty.

**BORACHIA**
My son slave!

**VICEROY**
Have you your wits?

**BORACHIA**
I'll not part with him so.

**CUCULO**
This I foresaw too.

**VICEROY**
Do not jest thyself
Into the danger of a father's anger.

**ALMIRA**
Jest, sir! by all my hope of comfort in him,
I am most serious. Good sir, look upon him;
But let it be with my eyes, and the care
You should owe to your daughter's life and safety,
Of which, without him, she's uncapable,
And you'll approve him worthy.

**VICEROY**
O thou shame
Of women! thy sad father's curse and scandal!
With what an impious violence thou tak'st from him,
His few short hours of breathing!

**PAULO**
Do not add, sir,
Weight to your sorrow in the ill-bearing of it.

**VICEROY**
From whom, degenerate monster, flow these low
And base affections in thee? what strange philtres
Hast thou received? what witch with damned spells
Deprived thee of thy reason? Look on me,
Since thou art lost unto thyself, and learn,
From what I suffer for thee, what strange tortures
Thou dost prepare thyself.

**DUKE of MESSINA**
Good sir, take comfort;
The counsel you bestow'd on me, make use of.

**PAULO**
This villain, (for such practices in that nation
Are very frequent,) it may be, hath forced,
By cunning potions, and by sorcerous charms,
This frenzy in her.

**VICEROY**
Sever them.

**ALMIRA**
I grow to him.

**VICEROY**
Carry the slave to torture, and wrest from him,
By the most cruel means, a free confession
Of his impostures.

**ALMIRA**
I will follow him,
And with him take the rack.

**BORACHIA**
No; hear me speak,
I can speak wisely: hurt not my son slave,
But rack or hang my husband, and I care not;
For I'll be bound body to body with him,
He's very honest, that's his fault.

**VICEROY**
Take hence
This drunken beast.

**BORACHIA**
Drunk! am I drunk? bear witness.

**CUCULO**
She is indeed distemper'd.

**VICEROY**
Hang them both,
If e'er more they come near the court.

**CUCULO**
Good sir,
You can recover dead men; can you cure
A living drunkenness?

**PAULO**
'Tis the harder task:
Go home with her, I'll send you something that
Shall once again bring her to better temper,
Or make her sleep for ever.

**CUCULO**
Which you please, sir.

[Exeunt **CUCULO** and **BORACHIA**.

**VICEROY**
Why linger you? rack him first, and after break him
Upon the wheel.

**PEDRO**
Sir, this is more than justice.

**ANTONIO**
Is't death in Sicily to be beloved
Of a fair lady?

**LEONORA**
Though he be a slave,
Remember yet he is a man.

**VICEROY**
I am deaf
To all persuasions: drag him hence.

[The **GUARD** carry off **ANTONIO**.

**ALMIRA**
Do, tyrant,
No more a father, feast thy cruelty
Upon thy daughter; but hell's plagues fall on me,

If I inflict not on myself whatever
He can endure for me!

**VICEROY**
Will none restrain her?

**ALMIRA**
Death hath a thousand doors to let out life,
I shall find one. If Portia's burning coals,
The knife of Lucrece, Cleopatra's aspics,
Famine, deep waters, have the power to free me
Prom a loath 'd life, I'll not an hour outlive him.

**PEDRO**
Sister!

**LEONORA**
Dear cousin!

[Exit **ALMIRA**, followed by **PEDRO** and **LEONORA**.

**VICEROY**
Let her perish.

**PAULO**
Hear me:
The effects of violent love are desperate,
And therefore in the execution of
The slave be not too sudden. I was present
When he was bought, and at that time myself
Made purchase of another; he that sold them
Said that they were companions of one country;
Something may rise from this to ease your sorrows.
By circumstance I'll learn what's his condition;
In the mean time use all fair and gentle means,
To pacify the lady.

**VICEROY**
I'll endeavour,
As far as grief and anger will give leave,
To do as you direct me.

**DUKE of MESSINA**
I'll assist you.

[Exeunt.

SCENE V. A Room in the Prison

[Enter **PEDRO** and **KEEPER**.

**PEDRO**
Hath he been visited already?

**KEEPER** Keep. Yes, sir,
Like one of better fortune; and to increase
My wonder of it, such as repair to him,
In their behaviour rather appear
Servants, than friends to comfort him.

**PEDRO**
Go fetch him.

[Exit **KEEPER**.

I am bound ingratitude to do more than wish
The life and safety of a man that hath
So well deserved me.

[Re-enter **KEEPER** with **ANTONIO** in his former dress, and **SERVANT**.

**KEEPER**
Here he is, my lord.

**PEDRO**
Who's here? thou art no conjurer to raise
A spirit in the best shape man e'er appeared in,
My friend, the prince of Tarent! doubts, forsake me!
I must and will embrace him.

**ANTONIO**
Pedro holds
One that loves life for nothing, but to live
To do him service.

**PEDRO**
You are he, most certain.
Heaven ever make me thankful for this bounty.
Run to the' Viceroy, let him know this rarity.

[Exit **KEEPER**.

But how you came here thus yet, since I have you,
Is't not enough I bless the prosperous means

That brought you hither?

**ANTONIO**
Dear friend, you shall know all;
And though, in thankfulness, I should begin
Where you deliver'd me

**PEDRO**
Fray you pass that over,
That's not worth the relation.

**ANTONIO**
You confirm
True friends love to do courtesies, not to hear them.
But I'll obey you. In our tedious passage
Towards Malta I may call it so, for hardly
We had lost the ken of Sicily, but we were
Becalm'd, and hull'd so up and down twelve hours;
When, to our more misfortunes, we descried '
Eight well-mann'd galleys making amain for us,
Of which the arch Turkish pirate, cruel
Dragut,
Was admiral: I'll not speak what I did
In our defence, but never man did more
Than the brave captain that you sent forth with me:
All would not do; courage oppress'd with number,
We were boarded, pillaged to the skin, and after
Twice sold for slaves; by the pirate first, and after
By a Maltese to signior Cuculo,
Which I repent 'not, since there 'twas my fortune
To be to you, my best friend, some ways useful
I thought to cheer you up with this short story,
But fou grow sad on't.

**PEDRO**
Have I not just cause,
When I consider I could be so stupid,
As not to see a friend through all disguises;
Or he so far to question my true love,
To keep himself conceal'd?

**ANTONIO**
Twas fit to do so,
And not to grieve you with the knowledge of
What then I was; where now I appear to you,
Your sister loving me, and Martino safe,
Like to myself and birth.

**PEDRO**
May you live long so!
How dost thou, honest friend? (your trustiest servant)
Give me thy hand: I now can guess by whom
You are thus furnish'd.

**ANTONIO**
Troth he met with me
As I was sent to prison, and there brought me
Such things as I had use of.

**PEDRO**
Let's to court,
My father never saw a man so welcome,
As you'll be to him.

**ANTONIO**
May it prove so, friend I

[Exeunt.


SCENE VI. A Room in the Viceroy's Palace

Enter **VICEROY, DUKE of MESSINA, CARDENES, PAULO, CAPTAIN, ALMIRA, LEONORA, WAITING-WOMEN,** and **ATTENDANTS.**

**VICEROY**
The slave changed to the prince of
Tarent, says he?

**CAPTAIN**
Yes, sir, and I the captain of the fort,
Worthy of your displeasure, and the effect oft,
For my deceiving of the trust your excellency
Reposed in me.

**PAULO**
Yet since all hath fallen out
Beyond your hopes, let me become a suitor,
And a prevailing one, to get his pardon.

**ALMIRA**
O, dearest Leonora, with what forehead
Dare I look on him now? too powerful Love,
The best strength of thy unconfined empire
Lies in weak women's hearts: thou art feign'd blind,

And yet we borrow our best sight from thee.
Could it be else, the person still the same,
Affection over me such power should have,
To make me scorn a prince, and love a slave?

**CARDENES**
But art thou sure 'tis he?

**CAPTAIN**
Most certain, sir.

**CARDENES**
Is he in health, strong, vigorous, and as able
As when he left me dead?

**CAPTAIN**
Your own eyes, sir,
Shall make good my report.

**CARDENES**
I am glad of it,
And take you comfort in it, sir, there's hope,
Fair hope left for me, to repair mine honour.

**DUKE of MESSINA**
What's that?

**CARDENES**
I will do something, that shall speak me
Messina's son.

**DUKE of MESSINA**
I like not this: one word, sir.

[Whispers the **VICEROY**.

**VICEROY**
We'll prevent it.
Nay, look up my Almira; now I approve
Thy happy choice; I have forgot my anger;
I freely do forgive thee.

**ALMIRA**
May I find
Such easiness in the wrong'd prince of Tarent!
I then were happy.

**LEONORA**

Rest assured you shall.

[Enter **ANTONIO, PEDRO,** and **SERVANT.**

**VICEROY**
We all with open arms haste to embrace you.

**DUKE of MESSINA**
Welcome, most welcome!

**CARDENES**
Stay.

**DUKE of MESSINA**
'Twas this I fear'd.

**CARDENES**
Sir, 'tis best known to you, on what strict terms
The reputation of men's fame and honours
Depends in this so punctual age, in which
A word that may receive a harsh construction,
Is answer'd and defended by the sword:
And you, that know so much, will, I presume,
Be sensibly tender of another's credit,
As you would guard your own.

**ANTONIO**
I were unjust else.

**CARDENES**
I have received from your hands wounds, and deep ones,
My honour in the general report
Tainted and soil'd, for which I will demand
This satisfaction that you would forgive
My contumelious words and blow, my rash
And unadvised wildness first threw on you.
Thus I would teach the world a better way.
For the recovery of a wounded honour,
Than with a savage fury, not true courage,
Still to run headlong on.

**ANTONIO**
Can this be serious?

**CARDENES**
I'll add this, he that does wrong, not alone
Draws, but makes sharp, his enemy's sword against
His own life and his honour. I have paid for't;

And wish that they who dare most, would learn from me,
Not to maintain a wrong, but to repent it.

**PAULO**
Why, this is like yourself.

**CARDENES**
For further proof,
Here, sir, with all my interest, I give up
This lady to you.

**VICEROY**
Which I make more strong
With my free grant.

**ALMIRA**
I bring mine own consent,
Which will not weaken it.

**OMNES**
All joy confirm it!

**ANTONIO**
Your unexpected courtesies amaze me,
Which I will study with all love and service
To appear worthy of.

**PAULO**
Pray you, understand, sir,
There are a pair of suitors more, that gladly
Would hear from you as much as the pleased viceroy
Hath said unto the prince of Tarent.

**DUKE of MESSINA**
Take her; her dowry shall be answerable to
Her birth, and your desert.

**PEDRO**
You make both happy.

**ANTONIO**
One only suit remains; that you would please
To take again into your highness' favour,
This honest captain: let him have your grace;
What's due to his much merit, shall from me
Meet liberal rewards.

**VICEROY**

Have your desire.

**ANTONIO**
Now may all here that love, as they are friends
To our good fortunes, find like prosperous ends.

[Exeunt.

EPILOGUE

Custom, and that a law we must obey,
In the way of epilogue bids me something say,
Howe'er to little purpose, since we know,
If you are pleased, unbeggd you will bestow
A gentle censure: on the other side,
If that this play deserve to be decried
In your opinions, all that I can say
Will never turn the stream the other way.
Your gracious smiles will render us secure;
Your frowns without despair we must endure.

PHILIP MASSINGER – A SHORT BIOGRAPHY

*This biography was initially written in 1830*

Very few materials exist for a life of Massinger beyond the entries of the Parish Register or the College Books, and a few slender intimations scattered here and there in the dedications to his plays. From these scanty sources the following brief memoir is derived.

Our author was born at Salisbury in the year 1584: he was the son of Arthur Massinger, a gentleman in the service of Henry, the second Earl of Pembroke. We must not suppose, from his being thus attached to the family of a nobleman, that the father of our poet was a person of inferior birth and station. In those days the word servant carried with it no sense of degradation. The great lords and officers of the court numbered inferior nobles among their followers. We read, in Cavendish's Life of Wolsey, that "my Lord Percy, the son and heir of the Earl of Northumberland, attended upon and was servitor to the lord-cardinal:" and from the situation which Arthur Massinger held in the household of so high and influential a person as the Earl of Pembroke, we might be justly led to argue rather favourably than unfavourably of his family and his connexions. "There were," says Mr. Gifford, "many considerations which united to render this state of dependance respectable and even honourable. The secretaries, clerks, and assistants, of various departments, were not then, as now, nominated by the government, but left to the choice of the person who held the employment; and as no particular dwelling was officially set apart for their residence, they were entertained in the house of their principal. That communication, too, between noblemen of power and trust, both of a public and private nature, which is now committed to the post, was in those days managed by confidential servants, who were despatched from one to the other, and even to the sovereign;" and, indeed, the father of our poet himself was, we know, in one instance thus employed as the bearer of communications from his patron to Elizabeth. We read in The Sidney Letters, "Mr. Massinger is newly come up from the Earl of Pembroke with letters to the queen for his lordship's leave to be away this St. George's Day." This was an errand which would not have been intrusted to the execution of any inconsiderable person: unimportant as the occasion may appear to us, it would not have been regarded in that light by Elizabeth; for no monarch ever exacted from the nobility, and particularly from her officers of state, a more rigid and scrupulous compliance with stated order than this princess.

With regard to the early youth of Massinger, we possess no information whatever. Mr. Gifford supposes that it might have been passed at Wilton, a seat belonging to the Earl of Pembroke, in the neighbourhood of Salisbury; but this mode of disposing of his early years rests on a very improbable conjecture. It may occasionally have happened that the child of a favourite dependant was admitted as the companion of the younger branches of the patron's family, and allowed to receive his education among them; but this was certainly not an ordinary case; and, like Cavendish, a large majority of the great man's servants and dependants "left wife and children, home and family, rest and quietness, only to serve him."—Massinger was most likely educated at the grammar-school of Salisbury, where many distinguished characters have received the rudiments of their education, among whom the elegant and accomplished Addison is to be numbered. But wherever the first years of our poet's life may have been spent, and whatever may have been the nature of his education, we know that at the age of eighteen (May 14, 1602) he was entered at the university of Oxford, and became a commoner of St. Alban's Hall.

Massinger resided at Oxford about four years, and then abruptly left it, without taking any degree. The cause of this sudden departure is ascribed by Mr. Gifford to the death of his father, from whom his supplies were derived: but Davies relates a very different story, and asserts that the Earl of Pembroke, who had sent him to the university and maintained him there, withdrew the necessary allowance in consequence of his having misapplied the time demanded for severer studies, in the pursuit of a more attractive but less profitable description of literature. Each opinion is equally ungrounded on the basis of any substantial evidence, and rests almost entirely on the imagination of the biographer: what slight authority there is favours the latter supposition, which, perhaps, on the whole, is most consistent with the known circumstances of the case. Anthony Wood, who was born, lived, and died at Oxford; who spent his time in collecting and recording the gossip which circulated in the university respecting the characters and conduct of its more distinguished sons; and whose evidence, however indifferent it may be, is the best that can be obtained upon the subject, confirms the representation of Davies:— "Massinger," says Wood, "gave his mind more to poetry and romance, for about four years or more, than to logic and philosophy, which he ought to have done, as he was patronised to that end." This passage corroborates the account of Davies so far as to intimate that patronage was afforded to our author, and that cause of dissatisfaction was given to the patron; but it goes no farther: it does not even state to whom the poet was indebted for assistance, nor that the misapplication of his academic hours was at all resented by the friend from whom the assistance was received: but still Wood is very probably correct in his information that other than his paternal funds were depended upon for maintaining Massinger at the university; and if such was the case, there can be no question from whose hands they must have proceeded; while the simple fact of his having been totally neglected, from the time of his father's death, by the whole of the Pembroke family, till after the demise of the earl, carries with it a strong suspicion that some offence was committed on the side of the poet, and tenaciously remembered on the side of the peer. Henry, the second Earl of Pembroke, died (1601) the year before Massinger was admitted at Oxford; and William, the third earl, to whom the father of Massinger continued attached during life, is universally and justly considered one of the brightest ornaments of the courts of Elizabeth and James. He was a man of generous and liberal disposition; the distinguished patron of arts and learning; and a lover of poetry, which he himself cultivated with some degree of success. It is not probable—it is impossible—that such a man should have allowed the highly talented son of an old and faithful servant of his family to be checked in his course of study, and abandoned to maintain, through the early years of life, a single-handed contest with adversity, for the want of that pecuniary aid which he could have yielded and never missed, unless some strong and decided cause of displeasure had existed. Had Massinger been merely forced to leave the university, as Mr. Gifford supposes, because the funds necessary to maintain him there had failed with the life of his father, we impute an act of illiberality to the Earl of Pembroke which is inconsistent with the whole tenor of his life and character. From whatever source the expenses of our author's education were originally defrayed, their suddenly ceasing argues in favour of the account intimated by Wood and detailed by Davies. If his father had, during his life, supported him at the university, there must have been some reason for the earl's not continuing that support when the father of Massinger was no more; and perhaps the most honourable supposition for both parties is that which represents the earl as offended by the bent of our author's studies and pursuits. By adopting this view of the case we are saved from the painful necessity of either assuming, on the one hand, that a nobleman distinguished among the most amiable characters of his age allowed a highly gifted and meritorious young man, a natural dependant of his house, to languish in the want of that countenance and protection on which he had an hereditary claim; or, on the other hand, that Massinger had incurred the displeasure of his natural and hereditary patron by the commission of some more crying offence.

Every, even the slightest, surmise of Mr. Gifford is deserving attention and respect; but I cannot admit the supposition by which he would account for the alienation that subsisted between the Earl of Pembroke and our author. That distinguished critic has inferred, from the religious sentiments contained in The Virgin Martyr, that Massinger was a Roman catholic, and for that cause neglected by the protector of his father. But if the intimations scattered through this play and others should be received as sufficient evidence of the faith of Massinger, we must, on similar evidence—the intimations contained in Measure for Measure, for instance—conclude that the religion of Shakspeare was the same; and then we are cast back upon our old difficulty, and have to explain why William Earl of Pembroke, a celebrated patron of literary men, and of dramatists in particular, scorned to yield his notice to the catholic Massinger, while (to use the expression of Heminge and Condell) he "prosequuted" the catholic Shakspeare and "his works with so much favour?" There are many reasons for believing Shakspeare to have been a member of the church of Rome; and the patronage afforded him by the Earl of Pembroke proves, that that nobleman extended his liberality to men of genius without any regard to distinctions of faith; but, on the other hand, we have no just grounds for assuming that Massinger really did hold the same opinions. The only evidence we have upon this point, that afforded by the general tone of his writings, is of a most vague and superficial description. What, in fact, can be inferred from it? We may from such a source derive very satisfactory information respecting the sentiments which would be favourably received by the audience, but very little respecting those of the author. The truth is, that though the national religion was reformed in its liturgy and articles, the feelings, prejudices, and superstitions of the people were still almost entirely catholic; and Massinger, like any other dramatic author, writing for the amusement of the people, necessarily addressed them in a language they would understand, and with sentiments that accorded with their own. Besides, as a poet, he would never carry his theological distinctions to his literary labours: Voltaire himself is catholic in his tragedies; and Massinger naturally adopted the creed which was most suitable to the purposes of poetry, and afforded the most picturesque ceremonies and romantic situations. I feel inclined, therefore, to dismiss entirely the theory suggested by Mr. Gifford, for these two reasons; first, supposing our author to have been a catholic, we have no reason for condemning the Earl of Pembroke as a bigot and a persecutor, who would close his eyes to the merits of so great an author, because his faith did not tally with his own; and, secondly, we have no sufficient grounds for supposing him to have been a catholic at all. But with regard to all such visionary conjectures, thinking is literally a waste of thought.

Whatever may have been the nature of Massinger's studies at Oxford, it is quite certain, from the general character of his works, that his time could not have been wasted there; and his literary acquirements, at the period of his leaving the university, appear to have been multifarious and extensive. He was about two-and-twenty (1606) when he arrived in London, where, as he more than once observes, he was driven by his necessities, and somewhat inclined, perhaps, by the peculiar bent of his talents, to dedicate himself to the service of the stage.

The theatre, when Massinger first took up his abode in the metropolis, must have presented attractions of all others the most calculated to excite the interest, and inspire the imagination, of a young man of sensibility, taste, and education like our poet. No art ever attained a more rapid maturity than the dramatic art in England. The people had, indeed, been long accustomed to a species of exhibition, called MIRACLES or MYSTERIES, founded on sacred subjects, and performed by the ministers of religion themselves, on the holy festivals, in or near the churches, and designed to instruct the ignorant in the leading facts of sacred history. From the occasional introduction of allegorical characters, such as Faith, Death, Hope, or Sin, into these religious dramas, representations of another kind, called MORALITIES, had by degrees arisen, of which the plots were more artificial, regular, and connected, and which were entirely formed of such personifications: but the first rough draught of a regular tragedy and comedy—Lord Sackville's Gorboduc, and Still's Gammer Gurton's Needle—were not produced till within the latter half of the sixteenth century, and little more than twenty years before the stage acquired its highest splendour in the productions of Shakspeare.

About the end of the sixteenth century, the attention of the public began to be more generally directed to the drama; and it throve most admirably beneath the cheering beams of popular favour. The theatrical performances which in the early part of Elizabeth's reign had been exhibited on temporary stages, erected in such halls or apartments as the actors could procure, or, more generally, in the yards of the larger inns, while the spectators surveyed them from the surrounding windows and galleries, began to find more convenient and permanent habitations. About the year 1569, a regular playhouse, under the appropriate name of The Theatre, was erected. It is supposed to have stood somewhere in Blackfriars; and, three years after the commencement of this establishment, the queen, yielding to her own inclination for such amusements, and disregarding the remonstrances of the Puritans, granted licence and authority to the servants of the Earl of Leicester ("for the recreation of her loving subjects, as for her own solace and pleasure when she should think good to see them") to exercise their occupation throughout the whole realm of England. From this time the number of theatres increased with the increasing demands of the people. Various noblemen had their respective companies of performers, who were associated as their servants, and acted under their protection; and when Massinger left Oxford, and commenced dramatic author, there were no less than seven principal theatres open in the metropolis.

With respect to the interior arrangements, there were very few points of difference between our modern theatres and those of the days of Massinger. The prices of admission, indeed, were considerably cheaper: to the boxes the entrance was a shilling; to the pit and galleries only sixpence. Sixpence also was the price paid for stools upon the stage; and these seats, as we learn from Decker's Gull's Hornbook, were particularly affected by the wits and critics of the time. The conduct of the audience was less restrained by the sense of public decorum, and smoking tobacco, playing at cards, eating and drinking, were generally prevalent among them. The hours of performance were also earlier: the play commencing at one o'clock. During the representation a flag was unfurled at the top of the theatre; and the stage, according to the universal practice of the age, was strewn with rushes; but, in all other respects, the theatres of Elizabeth and James's days seem to have borne a perfect resemblance to our own. They had their pit, where the inferior class of spectators, the groundlings, vented their clamorous censure or approbation; they had their boxes—rooms as they were called—to which the right of exclusive admission was engaged by the night, for the more affluent portion of the audience; and there were again the galleries, or scaffoldings above the boxes, for those who were content to purchase less commodious situations at a cheaper rate. On the stage, in the same manner, the appointments appear to have been nearly of the same description as at present. The curtain divided the audience from the actors, which, at the third sounding, not indeed of the bell, but of the trumpet, was drawn for the commencement of the performance. Malone, in his account of the ancient theatre, supposes that there were no moveable scenes; that a permanent elevation of about nine feet was raised at the back of the stage, from which, in many of the old plays, part of the dialogue was spoken; and that there was a private box on each side this platform. Such an arrangement would have destroyed all theatrical illusion; and it seems extraordinary that any spectators should desire to fix themselves in a station where they could have seen nothing but the backs and trains of the performers; but, as Malone himself acknowledges the spot to have been inconvenient, and that "it is not very easy to ascertain the precise situation where these boxes really were", it may very reasonably be presumed, that they were not placed in the position that the historian of the English stage has supposed. As to the permanent floor, or upper stage, of which he speaks, he may or may not be correct in his statement. All that his quotations upon the subject really establish is, that in the old, as in the modern theatre, when the actor was to speak from a window, or balcony, or the walls of a fortress, the requisite ingenuity was not wanting to contrive a representation of the place. But with regard to the use of painted moveable scenery, it is not possible, from the very circumstances of the case, to believe him correct in his theory. Such a contrivance could not have escaped our ancestors. All the materials were ready to their hands. They had not to invent for themselves, but merely to adapt an old invention to that peculiar purpose; and at a time when every better-furnished apartment was adorned with tapestry; when even the rooms of the commonest taverns were hung with painted cloths; while all the materials were constantly before their eyes, we can hardly believe our forefathers to have been so deficient in ingenuity, as to have missed the simple contrivance of converting the common ornaments of their walls into the decorations of their theatres. But, in fact, the use of scenery was almost co-existent with the introduction of dramatic representations in this country. In the Chester Mysteries (1268), the most ancient and complete collection of the kind which we possess, is found the following stage direction: "Then Noe shall go into the arke with all his familye, his wife excepte. The arke must be boarded round about; and upon the boardes all the beastes and fowles, hereafter rehearsed, must be painted, that their wordes may agree with their pictures." In this passage we have a clear reference to a painted scene. It is not likely that, in the lapse of three centuries, while all other arts were in a state of rapid improvement, and the art of dramatic writing, perhaps, more rapidly and successfully improved than any other, the art of theatrical decoration should have alone stood still. It is not improbable that their scenes were few; and that they were varied, as occasion might require, by the introduction of different pieces of stage furniture. Mr. Gifford, who adheres to the opinions of Malone, says, "A table with a pen and ink thrust in, signified that the stage was a counting-house; if these were withdrawn and two stools put in their place, it was then a tavern." And this might be perfectly satisfactory as long as the business of the play was supposed to be passing within doors; but when it was removed to the open air, such meagre devices would no longer be sufficient to guide the imagination of the audience, and some new method must have been adopted to indicate the place of action. After giving the subject very considerable attention, I cannot help thinking that Steevens was right in rejecting Malone's theory, and concluding that the spectators were, as at the present day, assisted in following the progress of the story by means of painted moveable scenery. This opinion is confirmed by the ancient stage directions. In the folio Shakspeare, 1623, we read "Enter Brutus in his orchard; Enter Timon in the woods; Enter Timon from the cave." In Coriolanus, "Marcius follows them to the gates and is shut in." Innumerable instances of the same kind might be cited to prove that the ancient stage was not so defective in the necessary decorations as some antiquaries of great authority would represent. "It may be added," says Steevens, "that the dialogue of our old dramatists has such perpetual reference to objects supposed visible to the audience, that the want of scenery could not have failed to render many of the descriptions absurd. Banquo examines the outside of Inverness castle with such minuteness, that he distinguishes even the nests which the martens had built under the projecting part of its roof. Romeo, standing in a garden, points to the tops of fruit-trees gilded by the moon. The prologue speaker to the second part of Henry the Fourth expressly shows the spectators 'This worm-eaten hold of ragged stone,' in which Northumberland was lodged. Iachimo takes the most exact inventory of every article in Imogen's bed-chamber, from the silk and silver of which her tapestry was wrought, down to the Cupids that support her andirons. Had not the inside of the apartment, with its proper furniture, been represented, how ridiculous must the action of Iachimo have appeared! He must have stood looking out of the room for the particulars supposed to be visible within it." The works of Massinger would afford innumerable instances of a similar kind to vindicate the opinion which Steevens has asserted on the testimony of Shakspeare alone. But on this subject there is one passage which appears to me quite conclusive. Must not all the humour of the mock play in The Midsummer Night's Dream have been entirely lost, unless the audience before whom it was performed were accustomed to all the embellishments requisite to give effect to a dramatic representation, and could consequently estimate the absurdity of those shallow contrivances and mean substitutes for scenery devised by the ignorance of the clowns?

In only one respect do I perceive any material difference between the mode of representation at the time of Massinger and at present: in his day, the female parts were performed by boys. This custom, which must in many cases have materially injured the illusion of the scene, was in others of considerable advantage: it furnished the stage with a succession of youths, regularly educated for the art, to fill, in every department of the drama, the characters suited to their age. When the lad had become too tall for Juliet, he had acquired the skill, and was most admirably fitted, both in age and appearance, for performing the part which Garrick considered the most difficult on the stage, because it needed "an old head upon young shoulders," the ardent and arduous character of Romeo. When the voice had "the mannish crack," that rendered the youth unfit to appear as the representative of the gentle Imogen, the stage possessed in him the very person that was wanting to do justice to the princely sentiments of Arviragus or Guiderius.

Such was the state of the stage when Massinger arrived in the metropolis, and dedicated his talents to its service. He joined a splendid fraternity, for Shakspeare, Jonson, Beaumont, Fletcher, Shirley, were then flourishing at the height of their reputation, and the full vigour of their genius. Massinger came among them no unworthy competitor for such honours and emoluments as the theatre could afford. Of the honours, indeed, he seems to have reaped a very fair and equitable portion; of the emoluments, the harvest was less abundant. In those days, very little pecuniary reward was to be gained by the dramatic poet, unless, as indeed was most frequently the case, he added the profession of the actor to that of the author, and recited the verses which he wrote. The distinguished performers of that time, Alleyn, Burbage, Heminge, Condell, Shakspeare, all appear to have died in independent, if not affluent, circumstances; but the remuneration obtained by the poet was most miserably curtailed. The price given at the theatre for a new play fluctuated between ten and twenty pounds; the copyright, if the piece was printed, might produce from six to ten pounds more; in addition to these sums, the dedication-fee may be reckoned, the usual amount of which was forty shillings. Our author appears to have produced about two or three plays every year. Most of them were successful; but, even with this industry and good fortune, his annual income would rarely have exceeded fifty pounds: and we cannot, therefore, feel surprised at finding him continually speaking of his necessities; or that the only existing document connected with his life should be one that represents him in a state of pecuniary embarrassment.

Among the papers of Dulwich College, the indefatigable Mr. Malone discovered the following letter tripartite, which, coming from persons of such deserved celebrity, cannot fail of interesting the reader.

"To our most loving friend, Mr. Phillip Hinchlow, esquire, these.

"Mr. Hinchlow,

"You understand our unfortunate extremitie, and I doe not thincke you so void of Christianitie but that you would throw so much money into the Thames as wee request now of you, rather than endanger so many innocent lives. You know there is xl. more, at least, to be receaved of you for the play. We desire you to lend us vl. of that, which shall be allowed to you; without which, we cannot be bayled, nor I play any more till this be dispatch'd. It will lose you xxl. ere the end of the next weeke, besides the hindrance of the next new play. Pray, sir, consider our cases with humanity, and now give us cause to acknowledge you our true freind in time of neede. Wee have entreated Mr. Davison to deliver this note, as well to witness your love as our promises, and alwayes acknowledgement to be ever

"Your most thankfull and loving friends,
"NAT. FIELD."

"The money shall be abated out of the money remayns for the play of Mr. Fletcher and ours.
"ROB. DABORNE."

"I have ever found you a true loving friend to mee, and in soe small a suite, it beinge honest, I hope you will not fail us.
"PHILIP MASSINGER."

Indorsed.
"Received by mee, Robert Davison, of Mr. Hinchlow, for the use of Mr. Daboerne, Mr. Feeld, Mr. Messenger, the sum of vl.
"ROB. DAVISON."

The occasion of the distress in which these three distinguished persons were involved it is not possible to fathom. We may imagine a thousand emergencies, either creditable or discreditable to the fame of the writers, with which the letter would perfectly tally; but, on such slight and vague intimations, no ingenuity could determine which was most likely to be correct. But from the document a circumstance is ascertained, which, before its discovery, had been called in question. Sir Aston Cockayne, a friend of Massinger, had asserted in a volume of poems, published in 1658, that our author had written in conjunction with Fletcher; Davies doubted this report, but the above letter establishes the fact beyond the possibility of dispute.

Massinger is known to have produced thirty-seven plays for the stage, a list of which is given at the conclusion of this memoir. Sixteen entire plays and the fragment of another, The Parliament of Love, alone are extant. No less than eleven of his productions, in manuscript, were in possession of Mr. Warburton (Somerset Herald), and destroyed with the rest of that gentleman's invaluable collection by his cook, who, ignorant of their worth, used them as waste paper for the purposes of the kitchen.

The great and various merits of the works of Massinger will be better seen in the following volumes than in any elaborate, critical dissertation. If our author be compared with the other dramatic writers of his age, we cannot long hesitate where to place him. More natural in his characters and more poetical in his diction than Jonson or Cartwright, more elevated and nervous than Fletcher, the only writers who can be supposed to contest his pre-eminence, Massinger ranks immediately under Shakspeare himself. Our poet excels, perhaps, more in the description than in the expression of passion; this may in some measure be ascribed to his attention to the fable: while his scenes are managed with consummate skill, the lighter shades of character and sentiment are lost in the tendency of each part to the catastrophe. The melody, force, and variety of his versification are always remarkable. The prevailing beauties of his productions are dignity and elegance; their predominant fault is want of passion.

Massinger's last play—which is unfortunately lost—The Anchoress of Pausilippo, was acted Jan. 26, 1640, about six weeks before his death, which happened on the 17th of March, 1640. He went to bed in good health, says Langbaine, and was found dead in the morning, in his own house on the Bankside. He was buried in the churchyard of St. Saviour's, and the comedians paid the last sad duty to his name, by attending him to the grave.

It does not appear, though every stone and every fragment of a stone has been carefully examined, that any monument or inscription of any kind marked the place where his dust was deposited. "The memorial of his mortality," says Gifford, "is given with a pathetic brevity, which accords but too well with the obscure and humble passages of his life: March 20, 1639-40, buried Philip Massinger, A STRANGER."

Such is all the information that remains to us of this distinguished poet. But though we are ignorant of every circumstance respecting him but that he lived, wrote, and died, we may yet form some idea of his personal character from the recommendatory poems prefixed to his several plays, in which, as Mr. Gifford justly observes, the language of his panegyrists, though warm, expresses an attachment apparently derived not so much from his talents as his virtues: he is their beloved, much-esteemed, dear, worthy, deserving, honoured, long-known, and long-loved friend. All the writers of his life represent him as a man of singular modesty, gentleness, candour, and affability; nor does it appear that he ever made or found an enemy.


PHILIP MASSINGER – A CONCISE BIBLIOGRAPHY

As would be expected many works from this time no longer exist either in part or their entirety. Further many playwrights collaborated on plays or revised them for later performances and we have used the latest position known on each of them for the bibliography below.

Solo Plays
The Maid of Honour, tragicomedy (c. 1621; printed 1632)

The Duke of Milan, tragedy (c. 1621–3; printed 1623, 1638)
The Unnatural Combat, tragedy (c. 1621–6; printed 1639)
The Bondman, tragicomedy (licensed 3 December 1623; printed 1624)
The Renegado, tragicomedy (licensed 17 April 1624; printed 1630)
The Parliament of Love, comedy (licensed 3 November 1624; MS)
A New Way to Pay Old Debts, comedy (c. 1625; printed 1632)
The Roman Actor, tragedy (licensed 11 October 1626; printed 1629)
The Great Duke of Florence, tragicomedy (licensed 5 July 1627; printed 1636)
The Picture, tragicomedy (licensed 8 June 1629; printed 1630)
The Emperor of the East, tragicomedy (licensed 11 March 1631; printed 1632)
Believe as You List, tragedy (rejected by the censor in January, but licensed 6 May 1631; MS)
The City Madam, comedy (licensed 25 May 1632; printed 1658)
The Guardian, comedy (licensed 31 October 1633; printed 1655)
The Bashful Lover, tragicomedy (licensed 9 May 1636; printed 1655)

Collaborations with John Fletcher
Sir John van Olden Barnavelt, tragedy (August 1619; MS)
The Little French Lawyer, comedy (c. 1619–23; printed 1647)
A Very Woman, tragicomedy (c. 1619–22; licensed 6 June 1634; printed 1655)
The Custom of the Country, comedy (c. 1619–23; printed 1647)
The Double Marriage, tragedy (c. 1619–23; Printed 1647)
The False One, history (c. 1619–23; printed 1647)
The Prophetess, tragicomedy (licensed 14 May 1622; printed 1647)
The Sea Voyage, comedy (licensed 22 June 1622; printed 1647)
The Spanish Curate, comedy (licensed 24 October 1622; printed 1647)
The Lovers' Progress or The Wandering Lovers, tragicomedy (licensed Dec 1623; rev 1634; printed 1647)
The Elder Brother, comedy (c. 1625; printed 1637).

Collaborations with John Fletcher and Francis Beaumont
Thierry and Theodoret, tragedy (c. 1607; printed 1621)
The Coxcomb, comedy (1608–10; printed 1647)
Beggars' Bush, comedy (c. 1612–15; revised 1622; printed 1647)
Love's Cure, comedy (c. 1612–15; revised 1625; printed 1647).

Collaborations with John Fletcher and Nathan Field
The Honest Man's Fortune, tragicomedy (1613; printed 1647)
The Queen of Corinth, tragicomedy (c. 1616–18; printed 1647)
The Knight of Malta, tragicomedy (c. 1619; printed 1647).

Collaborations with Nathan Field
The Fatal Dowry, tragedy (c. 1619, printed 1632); adapted by Nicholas Rowe: The Fair Penitent

Collaborations with John Fletcher, John Ford, and William Rowley, or John Webster
The Fair Maid of the Inn, comedy (licensed 22 January 1626; printed 1647).

Collaborations with John Fletcher, Ben Jonson, and George Chapman
Rollo Duke of Normandy, or The Bloody Brother, tragedy (c. 1616–24; printed 1639).

Collaborations with Thomas Dekker
The Virgin Martyr, tragedy (licensed 6 October 1620; printed 1622).

Collaborations with Thomas Middleton and William Rowley
The Old Law, comedy (c. 1615–18; printed 1656).

www.ingramcontent.com/pod-product-compliance
Lightning Source LLC
Chambersburg PA
CBHW060115050426
42448CB00010B/1874